MARY, QUEEN of SCOTS
and ALL HER GHOSTS

JOYCE MILLER and MARTIN COVENTRY

GOBLINSHEAD

First Published 2013
© Joyce Miller and Martin Coventry

Published by GOBLINSHEAD
130B Inveresk Road, Musselburgh EH21 7AY, Scotland
Tel: 0131 665 2894
Email: goblinshead@sol.co.uk

ISBN 9781899874514

Typeset by GOBLINSHEAD using DTP
Printed by Bell & Bain, Glasgow

If you would like a full colour leaflet of our books on Scottish history,
travel, castles and the supernatural, please contact us at:
Goblinshead, 130B Inveresk Road
Musselburgh EH21 7AY, Scotland
Tel: **0131 665 2894**
Email: **goblinshead@sol.co.uk**

Written, printed and published in Scotland

CONTENTS

HOW TO USE THE BOOK

The book is divided into four sections:

- Narrative of Mary's life and events surrounding her reign, abdication, imprisonment and execution (pages 1–85). A family tree explains the relationship between the Royal houses of Stewart, Tudor and Valois (page 20).

- Mary's legacy and reputation examines how Mary's life and death has been recast, re-examined and portrayed (pages 86-94).

- Detailed accounts of ghost stories associated with Mary and other related historical personalities, from Scotland, England and beyond (pages 95-127).

- Places to visit which have either reported sightings of Mary's spirit, have a particular association with her but appear not to be haunted, or have interesting tales of other ghostly manifestations (pages 130-156) listing over 60 castles, palaces, houses, abbeys and museums. Information includes location, a brief description and summary of any ghostly activity, opening times, access, facilities, and contact details.

Two maps (pages 128-129) locate the sites.

An index (pages 157-163) lists main people, events, places, battles and ghosts.

INTRODUCTION

Why write a book about Mary? Has it not all been said before in less detail, more detail, with fewer pictures, with more pictures, for children, for adults, for tourists, for academics…slice her, dice her, chop her head off, serve her any which way you like, but surely the life of Mary Queen of Scots and all that, has been done to death?

Yes but wait a minute, what about **after** her death? Mary died in 1587 but her reputation and myth really only started after her execution, when rival accounts of her life portrayed her as either incompetent and guilty or unfortunate and innocent. Later biographies, dramas, operas, novels, films, plays, paintings and other stories sustained this dichotomy, this paradox, and this conflict within Mary's own story. It was further increased by adding to the mix a deliberate and sharp contrast with Elizabeth, as these two queens could not have been more different.

However, one area that has not been covered before, and which has revealed interesting insights into reactions and responses to Mary's life and story, are the numerous tales of ghosts or ghostly manifestations that have been identified as being Mary. From Borthwick Castle in Midlothian to Bolton Castle in Yorkshire, from female figures wearing black dresses to balls of light, many accounts about Mary's spirit have been recorded and continue to circulate.

Reports of Mary's spirit in a variety of forms have been documented in more than 25 sites in Scotland and in England, and show a continued, and continuing, interest in her story. It is clear that whatever opinion one has of Mary's life, her captivity and dramatic death enhanced her reputation; indeed for some her end perhaps cancelled out her mistakes and poor judgement. Stories about manifestations of her restless spirit, in places where she was held against her will, slot easily into the canon of myths and legends about Mary and have without a doubt contributed to the enduring nature of her legacy.

As ever with books about ghost stories, we do not make any claims about the reality or otherwise of stories about dead spirits, but repeat them here to illustrate the similarities between the descriptions, to place them in the historical and physical context of Mary's life, and to propose that these accounts have a claim to be part of her story. They are really orally transmitted, folk tales, which have been used to memorialize Mary's death. They may well have been inspired by written accounts that portrayed her as a martyr and victim, but nevertheless appear to have developed a legitimacy and momentum of their own.

We make no judgement about those who claim to have seen or felt some form of spirit activity. Academic studies have shown around 30% of people believe in ghosts, and around 15% claim to have experienced some form of spiritual activity; the majority either don't believe or are undecided. Those who believe will interpret experiences differently from those who don't, but what is interesting is the fact that these kinds of stories prove popular – even amongst sceptics. I can quite honestly say that I have never seen or felt any ghost of Mary Queen of Scots, but then I have visited sites during the day, in the presence of staff and other members of the public; at night (or early morning or evening), with no-one around, the atmosphere and conditions are bound to be very different. Having chatted with custodians at various sites over the years, a number of them have told us about experiencing 'interesting' sensations at quiet times (morning or early evening). Nothing specific, but then again…

Some of the stories of Mary's ghostly apparitions appear to be have been recorded in the 19th century and later, after the production of historical, romanticised versions of Mary's life; they may even have been the inspiration for some so-called manifestations. Some accounts have been publicised and reported quite enthusiastically, possibly for financial gain or notoriety; other sources or locations prefer to maintain a keen sense of scepticism. A few claims appear to have very little in the way of plausible explanation or connection with Mary at all, yet are still repeated quite regularly. It would seem therefore that, for the most part, having a resident Mary Queen of Scots ghost (fictional or otherwise) mostly does a place no harm, and may even bring in a few more visitors.

LIST OF ILLUSTRATIONS

Photographs by Martin Coventry, Joyce Miller, Dorothy Miller or Kay Miller.
Maps by © Martin Coventry,

ACKNOWLEDGEMENTS

Thanks to everyone who helped with the book, and especially to:
Dorothy and **Kay Miller** for making trips into the unknown... Also
many thanks for all their help to Ian Forbes, Diane Naylor, Christine
Reynolds, Katie Boggis, Jo Pritchard and Harriette Evans, Marie Louise
Larsson, Shona Sinclair and Derek Lunn, Stephen at the Covenanter
Hotel, Gemma Anderson, Philip Hunt and Hannah Kendall.

COLOUR SECTION
Ian Forbes at Blairs Museum for the portraits of Mary (pages 1 and 13)
Shona Sinclair at Scottish Borders Council and **Derek Lunn** for the
death mask of Mary and interior shot of Mary Queen of Scots Visitor
Centre (page 3 and 14); **Katie Boggis** at Bolton Castle for the shot of
Bolton (page 5); **National Portrait Gallery,** London for
Queen Elizabeth I c.1575 (page 6); **Diane Naylor**, Chatsworth for portrait
believed to be of Mary Queen of Scots, Alonso Sanchez Coello (page 7);
Marie Louise Larsson at Dragsholm Slot for the picture of the castle
(page 9); **Philip Hunt** at the Picture Library of the National Galleries of
Scotland for James Hepburn, 4th Earl of Bothwell, study of mummified
head (page 9) and *Execution of Mary Queen of Scots* (page 12); **Jo Pritchard**
and **Harriette Evans** at Tutbury Castle for the photo of the castle (page
10); **Christine Reynolds**, The Library, Westminster Abbey for the
picture of Mary's tomb (page 14); **Neil Fraser** at RCAHMS Enterprises
and Lennoxlove House for the death mask of Mary Queen of Scots (page
15); **Hannah Kendall** at the Ashmolean Museum for *Study for the
Execution of Mary Queen of Scots*, Ford Madox Brown (page 16).

MAIN TEXT
Katie Boggis at Bolton Castle for the Mary's bedroom at Bolton (page
67); **Jo Pritchard** and **Harriette Evans** at Tutbury Castle for the photos
of the castle (page 75 and 154); **Christine Reynolds**, The Library,
Westminster Abbey for the picture of Mary's effigy (page 82); **Gemma
Anderson** at Melville Castle for the photos of the castle (page 100);
Stephen from Covenanter Hotel, Falkland, for photo of the hotel (page
102); **Marie Louise Larsson** at Dragsholm Slot for the picture of the
castle (page 127).

MARY, QUEEN of SCOTS and ALL HER GHOSTS

IN MY END IS MY BEGINNING

So embroidered Mary Queen of Scots on her cloth of state, as she neared death on the orders of her cousin, and fellow queen, Elizabeth I of England. Mary also incorporated the emblem of the phoenix, a mythological bird reborn in the ashes of its predecessor, which was used by her mother Mary of Guise into her work. Was Mary deliberately implying that her death would start the rebirth of her reputation? If so, her prediction has come true in many ways. Since her execution at Fotheringhay in 1587, Mary has been the subject of much discussion, speculation and assertion, in particular about numerous sightings of ghosts or spectres in places associated with her – and some with which she had no particular association in life. It would seem that whilst she spent many of her adult years in restricted custody in England, her ghost is allegedly one of the most hard-working and ubiquitous in the country – stories about ghosts and spectres which are claimed to be Mary are recorded for around 30 sites in Scotland and England, although seem of these are – to say the least – speculative, even for ghost stories.

Why are there so many stories and legends about Mary? Was it because she has been presented either as a tragic martyr or a foolish failure? Since her death, as in life, Mary has proven to be an enigma, someone who has attracted as much praise and admiration, as criticism and condemnation. Her life, her loves, her captivity, her plotting, her death, her gender, have all proved grist to the mill of writers, poets, historians, painters, and dramatists who have offered varied accounts of her actions and decisions and those of the many other people involved with her. Indeed, rather than being remembered as a jealous and dangerous Catholic threat to the security and legitimacy of Protestant England and Elizabeth, as portrayed by Elizabeth's secretary Cecil, Mary's reputation as a martyr to her Catholic faith started with her execution. Her personal rule of her kingdom of Scotland, which even to the most generous of supporters was hardly a great success, has been recast as demonstrating a desire for tolerance and mediation – not something that found much acceptance in the disruptive years of 16th-century Reformation Scotland.

Mary inherited the crown of Scotland at just six days of age. The country then experience the wrath of Henry VIII and war with England which forced the Scottish political elite to send her, aged five, to the safety of her Guise-Lorraine relatives and ultimately the Valois court in France. She spent 13 years in France, much of the time in preparation for her future role as queen of France. After a brief time as queen of France and Scotland,

Mary (François Clouet)

which included an ambitious if rather politically injudicious claim to be queen of England by her father-in-law, Mary returned reluctantly to her first kingdom where she ruled in her own right for a short and dramatic six years. The next 19 years were spent in various castles and houses in England while Elizabeth and Cecil debated her fate.

It would seem that despite there being so many known facts about Mary's life, there are also many unknowns: why did she not convert to Protestantism? Why did she appear to consent to the murder of Darnley, given that he was probably in the terminal stage of syphilis? Why did she marry Bothwell? Why did she agree to abdicate? Why did she flee to England rather than face her Scottish opponents? Why did she write compromising letters to Catholic plotters when she knew her correspondence was being read? Why did she burst into tears so often? Why was she not more like Elizabeth?

Mary appears to us through many conflicting and contrived, written and visual portrayals, but she is still mostly quite invisible and unknowable. Her many ghosts, therefore, may be a metaphor and explanation for her invisibility and mystery, which transcend her contradictory and very public, reputation. Perhaps they result from pity or guilt about the circumstances of her death. Perhaps they derive from Mary's own behaviour at her execution and her desire to convey an image of dignity and strength to be used as propaganda. Perhaps they result from her transformation into a Catholic martyr, with pilgrimages to her effigy, claims of miracles and intercessions, and campaigns to have her canonised.

On the other hand, they may just be good stories…

SCOTLAND BEFORE MARY
JAMES IV AND JAMES V

On 14 November 1542, the year of Mary's birth, James V – her father – followed his more popular father's example by commanding a Scottish army to yet another major defeat by the English, this time at Solway Moss. In the event, relatively few Scots were killed, but 1200 were taken prisoner and it was not to James's credit that so many of his troops preferred to surrender than to die for their king. James himself died a month later, from cholera or dysentery.

The battle at Solway Moss may not have resulted in such a huge loss of life as Flodden in 1513, but the causes and consequences of the battle were just as serious for the kingdom and the Scots. In 1513, James IV had led his army to face the English because of complex European politics but also because of James IV's own opinion of himself as the brightest and best of the Stewart kings. He had charisma, bravery, and political ability as well as intelligence and cultural sophistication. He was an energetic king, who undertook his royal responsibilities well, attending and dispensing justice and holding regular parliaments – at least in the early years of his reign. He built up a navy and ensured the Scottish army of common men were regularly

Falkland Palace

mustered. He maintained an elegant and cultured Renaissance court; founded a university in Aberdeen; built royal palace blocks at Stirling, Falkland and Linlithgow and spoke many languages.

He had also supported Perkin Warbeck, pretender to the English crown, against Henry VII in 1496. Their Northumberland campaign gained little in the way of territory for James, and for Warbeck would prove fatal as he was later executed for treason. But for the Scottish king it was a useful symbolic success: James and Henry agreed to the Treaty of Perpetual Peace and James gained a bride in the shape of Margaret, Henry's daughter. Henry VII had had to divert his resources to address a rising in Cornwall, which may have contributed to his abandonment of his northern defence in 1497, nevertheless by 1503 James IV and the Stewarts were very close to the Tudor line which itself, having been founded by Henry VII, was not overly secure.

When Henry VIII succeeded his father in 1509 James IV was his heir, however James preferred to maintain good diplomatic relations with France. Relations between Louis VII and Pope Julius II were strained and James IV cast himself as a go-between and mediator by expressing his desire to go on crusade. However, when the Holy League, which included Henry VIII, declared war against France, James allied with Louis. Following Henry's invasion of northern France in 1513, James sent 13 ships including the *Great Michael* to help the French. While Henry was occupied in France, James once again led his army into Northumberland. But this was not to be a repeat of the 1496-7 campaign. Henry had left Thomas, Earl of Surrey, ready to summon an army if needed – and Henry's first wife Catherine of Aragon provided more support. On 9 September 1513, James and the Scots, for once, outnumbered the English (35,000 to 26,000) and were in a better strategic position on Flodden Hill. However, the Scots abandoned their key position and moved to Branxton Hill, where the more experienced English defeated Scottish equipment and tactics. There was a heavy loss of life: 10,000 Scots (and an unknown number of English: perhaps a handful up to 4,000) but perhaps most seriously, James was killed, along with nine earls, 14 lesser lords, the archbishop of St Andrews, the bishops of Caithness and the Isles, two abbots, the French ambassador and many more ordinary men and foot soldiers. According to legend, Catherine sent James IV's blood-stained shirt to Henry, who was campaigning in France.

The flowers of the forest were all wede away in the space of an autumn afternoon: the king and most of the Scottish elite had all been slain, and from being a secure and flourishing court and kingdom, Stewart Scotland was once again faced with a hiatus of power and a child monarch. James V was only 17 months old and rivalries and disputes about regents and custody of the king, as well as the loss of a generation of the political elite, did little to restore peace and security to the country quickly.

Because James V was so young, the country experienced the factionalism associated with rule by regents, particularly the rivalry between the Hamiltons and the Douglases. From 1525, Archibald Douglas, Earl of Angus, dominated both the country and the young king until James escaped in 1528. James fled to Stirling, and Angus and his Douglas relatives were forced out of government. Despite surviving a royal siege of the Douglas stronghold of Tantallon Castle in East Lothian, Angus was eventually exiled

Tantallon Castle

to England. Several other members of the Douglas family were not treated quite so leniently: Janet, Lady Glamis, was burnt having been accused of murdering her husband using poison and witchcraft, but her real crime was that she was Angus's sister.

Aspects of James V's personal rule reflected that of his father: James V spent lavishly, rebuilding royal residences and patronising writers and musicians – in particular Sir David Lindsay of the Mount and Robert Carver. He restored law and order throughout the kingdom and inaugurated the College of Justice in 1532, attending and participating in justice ayres and raids, especially in the border areas. Johnny Armstrong was one infamous Border reiver whose execution was witnessed by the king.

In common with his father, James V needed money to pay for his building work and legal reforms, and one area he exploited was revenue from the church. Schismatic events in England had led to Henry VIII replacing the authority of the Pope with his own during the early 1530s and reforming ideas were impacting in other areas in Europe. All of which gave Scotland, and James, a bargaining position with Pope Clement VII who agreed to James's demands for monetary rewards in return for remaining loyal to the Catholic faith and church. Indeed James's policies, supported by Cardinal Beaton, towards supporters of Lutheran and other Protestant ideas, were severe: execution by burning. There was also the little matter of a cash payment to James (£72,000) and access to the revenue from the lands and estates of the wealthy abbeys and the filling of benefice positions with his illegitimate sons. Like his father before him, James V had several mistresses and illegitimate children, one of whom, Lord James Stewart (later Earl of Moray) would later play a significant role in Mary's reign.

James V's dealings with international politics also compared quite favourably with his father's. The Auld Alliance was maintained, and at the same time James kept peace with England – at least until his mother died in 1541. Despite several other possibilities and some hostility to the idea, he successfully negotiated two French marriages, which naturally meant two dowries. James acquired several honours from England and France – the Garter, St Michael and the Golden Fleece – as 'rewards' during these

James V's honours, Linlithgow Palace

negotiations during which time Henry VIII had also made suggestions to James regarding his support for Reformation. In 1536, before James married, Henry had invited him to England. James agreed to this, against the advice of his privy council, but then travelled to France, making it clear his bride of choice would be French and Catholic.

James V's first wife Madeleine, daughter of François I of France, died shortly after her arrival in Scotland; his second was Mary of Guise-Lorraine, from the very powerful Guise-Lorraine family. Mary had also been suggested for Henry VIII after Jane Seymour died and her preference for James was perhaps another irritant for Henry. Mary and James also added insult to injury with the birth of two sons in 1540 and 1541. Although both died in 1542, Mary fell pregnant again.

Henry had dissolved the wealthy monastic houses in England and supplemented his royal income greatly as a result and he proposed to James that he should enforce a similar scheme in Scotland. James seemed sufficiently impressed and again agreed to meet Henry at York in 1541. Although there were a number of pro-English sympathisers in Scotland, James's council prevented him from travelling south as they feared Henry would either kidnap James or persuade him to convert to Protestantism. James's 'no show' was another great insult to Henry, who had travelled to York — no mean feat given his physical condition — and it did not sit well with the English king.

As the shifting sands of international alliances altered, Henry allied with Charles V, the Holy Roman Emperor, against France again. Anglo-Scottish relations also cooled after the debacle at York and Henry revived ancient claims of English overlordship of Scotland. In autumn 1542 he mustered his troops for an invasion, led by Sir Robert Bowes and supported by the exiled Earl of Angus and others of the Douglas family. However despite initial successes by the English, Scottish troops led by George Gordon, the Earl of Huntly, and the Earl of Home, ambushed a party of Englishmen and chased them back to their main camp at Haddon Rig, near Berwick. At the battle the Scots were victorious, and took about 600 prisoners, killing another 400 including Bowes himself. The Scots failed to capitalize on their advantages, and lack of provisions contributed to a discontented army. James, instead of working with the victorious Huntly, blamed him for 'inaction' and replaced him with the Earl of Moray, as a result alienating some of the other nobles.

Henry's response was to send an even greater number of men north and James decided to launch an offensive action. It was late in the campaign season but James left Edinburgh, leaving Moray with some troops at Haddington in East Lothian, and advanced to Lochmaben near Dumfries, in the southwest, with the rest of his army to meet up with more Scottish troops, led by Robert Lord Maxwell. The skirmish took place at Solway Moss on 14 November 1542, with the Scots in a poor strategic position between a damp place and a wet place: a bog and a river.

After his defeat, James headed back via Peebles to Edinburgh, spent a week at Linlithgow with his queen, who was in the late stages of pregnancy, then left for Falkland Palace in Fife. It was there he took to his bed, a broken, disappointed man, with no physical injuries but very possibly suffering from cholera or dysentery. According to John Knox's account of his deathbed scene, when news came in December that Mary of Guise was delivered of a girl, James (allegedly) responded with the words 'it cam wi a lass and it'll gang wi a lass'. With the death of her father on 14 December, Scotland was left with a six-day old queen, a vacuum of power, and an aggressive and powerful king in England. Although the next few years would prove to be complicated and eventful, the rest of Mary's life would continue along similar lines.

Whilst James V has often been cast as one of the least successful and unpopular of Stewart monarchs, much of this character assassination came from the pens of later Protestant writers, including John Knox, whose agenda was to criticise James's support for Catholicism and punishment of Protestant heretics. Events may have turned out very differently had James not been defeated and died in 1542, but it would be quite likely that hostilities with England would have continued much as they did during Mary's early years.

Falkland Palace, James V died here in 1542.

AN INFANT QUEEN
MARY'S FIRST FIVE YEARS

When Mary was born at Linlithgow on 8 December 1542, her birth was not greeted with great celebration. Yes, Mary of Guise had been delivered safely of a live child, but the child was female. Female monarchs ruling in their own right were exceptional in 16th-century Europe. Her father, having lost to the English at Solway Moss the previous month, died six days later leaving his kingdom and his infant daughter the objects of Henry VIII's ambition. In the following years, Europe would continue to be riven by religious and political strife as a consequence of the Reformation, and Scotland would be no exception. Mary could not have known it, but her life was never going to be straightforward.

Mary was baptised soon after her father's funeral and the governing of the kingdom was to be done by James Hamilton, Earl of Arran, who was also James II's great-grandson and so was Mary's heir. Cardinal Beaton was appointed chancellor. As Arran was a Protestant, he negotiated a peace with Henry in July 1543, which included a betrothal contract between the infant queen and Henry's son Edward. The Treaty of Greenwich was not popular

Linlithgow Palace, Mary was born here in 1542.

with others of the Scottish political elite, particularly Cardinal Beaton. Mary was crowned at Stirling on 9 September 1543, and the Treaty of Greenwich was cancelled by the Scottish parliament by the end of the year. The rejection of the treaty led to a revival of Catholic power in Scotland, led by Cardinal Beaton and Mary of Guise. Their supporters included Huntly, Lennox, Argyll and Bothwell. The ever-vacillating Arran also embraced the old faith, and joined Beaton and Mary of Guise. In retaliation for the behaviour of the Scots, Henry ordered a series of raids into Scotland during 1544 and 1545, mainly in the border area, but also as far north as Edinburgh. These raids, later given the title the 'Rough Wooing' by Walter Scott, were led by the Earl of Hertford, and resulted in the looting and burning of the abbeys at Holyrood, Melrose, Jedburgh, Kelso and Dryburgh. Crops and ships were also stolen. Henry's orders were quite explicit:

> ...Put all to fyre and sworde, burne Edinborough towne, so rased and defaced when you have sacked and gotten what ye can of it, as there may remayn forever a perpetual memory of the vengeaunce of God lightened upon them for their faulsehode and disloyailtye.

During the first few years of her life, Mary had been brought up with her half-brothers and sisters, Lord James, Lord Robert and Lady Jean Stewart, speaking Scots, well away from the day-to-day problems of the country. As well as assuring her future as queen of Scots, her mother had Mary's immediate future survival to consider, as the threat from England persisted. There was also the real and present danger that Henry planned to kidnap the infant queen and force the marriage contract. For her safety, Mary was kept at Stirling Castle until the disastrous defeat at Pinkie, near Musselburgh, in September 1547. The Scots had defeated a force of English at Ancrum Moor in early 1545, but this was only a short-lived victory. With the death of Henry in January 1547, the English crown passed to Edward VI, who was, like Mary, a minor, so the Earl of Hertford, now the Duke of Somerset, who built forts in the south-east of Scotland from Berwick to Dundee, was in charge and concentrated his English troops at Haddington. He engaged the Scots in battle at Pinkie, near Musselburgh, on 9 September 1547. The Earl of Arran led the Scots' army, and there were reportedly 30,000 men drawn from throughout kingdom. Unfortunately, although the Scots outnumbered the English, the English were more professionally organized, trained and equipped, and by the end of the fighting 10,000 Scots were dead and a further 1,500 taken prisoner. Pinkie was an important victory for the English; they took Haddington and had Edinburgh in their sights. Dunbar Castle

Falside Castle, which overlooked the battlefield and was burnt.

was burnt, as were Musselburgh and Dalkeith. Hostilities between the two countries were to continue for another three years, and contributed to increased Scottish dependency on France.

At the time of the Rough Wooing other cataclysmic events were taking place that would have long-term effects on European society. Throughout the 16th century, the Reformation affected the whole of Europe: politics, culture, alliances, economy, were all changed. In Scotland, Lutheran ideas and literature had been imported into the eastern ports of Aberdeen, Dundee, Leith and St Andrews. Much ink has been spilt analysing whether the Scottish Reformation was a result of dissatisfaction with the Catholic church, which was accused of corruption and greed, or an increased desire for individual spirituality and responsibility advocated by Protestantism. Whatever the reasons, during Mary's minority rule, the 1540s and 1550s, there was as much religious as political unrest in Scotland.

Cardinal David Beaton, as Archbishop of St Andrews, was head of the church in Scotland and as he supported Catholic policies in Scotland, Beaton was seen as a major opponent to Henry. Like many other churchmen of the time, he had a mistress by whom he had three children; the practice of celibacy by clerics was not officially sanctioned by the church until the final debates of the Council of Trent in 1564. Beaton built Melgund Castle, near Brechin, for his family. Although Beaton may not have ordered the burning of as many heretics as in some other countries, he still sent several to the stake, most importantly George Wishart. The burning of Wishart at St Andrews in 1546 may have been a turning point for the Reformation in Scotland, and it was certainly to prove very serious for Beaton himself. As a result of this execution, Norman Leslie, James Melville, Kirkcaldy of Grange and some others stole into St Andrews Castle, where Beaton was in residence, and murdered him. His naked dead body was hung from one of the windows to demonstrate what had been done in retaliation for Wishart's death.

The removal of Beaton from the political and religious scene did not lead to any real change in Scottish politics and religion. Mary of Guise's own personal authority increased and, as a result of her influence, Arran ordered St Andrews Castle to be besieged. The siege might have resulted in a humiliating defeat for Mary and Arran as the castle was provided with enough food and ammunition to withstand an attack of several months. Among the besieged was John Knox, who would court controversy on several occasions in the future. The mine and counter-mine, which were tunnelled under St Andrews Castle during the siege, can still be seen. The stalemate was not broken, with the English reinforcing the Castilians, until the French arrived in 1547. The French king François I had died and his successor, Henri II, had placed the Duke of Guise and the Cardinal of Lorraine, Mary of Guise's brothers, in positions of power. The French sent a fleet of 20 ships whose

St Andrews Castle

ordnance was to prove successful against the English troops and the Castilians. The defeated Protestants were taken away, some to prison in France and others as galley slaves.

Mary had been moved from Stirling Castle to Inchmahome Priory, in Stirlingshire, then to Dumbarton Castle. In July 1548, French troops landed at Leith and advanced towards Haddington to help the Scots defeat the English. On 7 July the Scots and French signed the Treaty of Haddington, which promised a marriage between Mary and the dauphin François. Mary's mother clearly favoured a renewal of the French alliance for the protection of her daughter and her adopted kingdom. Arran, who had hoped for a possible union between Mary and his son James, had to be persuaded to agree. The offer of a French duchy with an annual pension seemed to do the trick, and Arran consented to the French marriage. He took the title Duke of Châtelherault in 1549 and remained the heir apparent. Mary sailed for France from Dumbarton on 7 August 1548 and arrived at Roscoff in Brittany six days later.

Several attendants embarked with Mary. The Lords Erskine and Livingston were sent as her guardians, Jean Sinclair as her nurse, and Lady Fleming as her governess. As companions she had the sons and daughters of Scottish nobility, including the Four Marys – Fleming, Livingston, Seton and Beaton. Mary Fleming was related to the royal house of Stewart through her mother. Mary Beaton was the daughter of the murdered Cardinal Beaton. Mary Seton's father was Lord Seton, who was to remain loyal to Mary throughout her life, and Mary Livingston was the daughter of Lord Livingston. Because of their noble birth they were acceptable as ladies-in-waiting for the future queen of France.

Inchmahome Priory

FRENCH QUEEN IN TRAINING

Mary arrived at Roscoff and would remain in France for the next 13 years. In retrospect, these years may have been Mary's happiest. Compared to her life after 1561, they were carefree and comfortable. Under the protection of her French grandparents Claud and Antoinette, Duke and Duchess of Guise, her half-brother François Duke of Longueville from her mother's first marriage, and many other uncles and aunts of the powerful Guise-Lorraine family, Mary could, perhaps for the first time, freely enjoy the splendour and pleasures of court life.

The Guise court may not have been the Valois court, but to all intents and purposes the power and influence emanating from this extended dynasty was impressive. It was here that Mary started her education proper; having been brought up speaking Scots she now had to learn French, and eventually mastered Latin, Italian, Spanish and Greek. She participated enthusiastically in music and dancing – playing the lute – and writing poetry, something she would continue to do throughout her adult life. Mary also became an accomplished horsewoman and enjoyed riding and hunting. She was trained to be a French princess, becoming fully immersed in this new environment. Throughout the rest of her life Mary appeared to be more comfortable with her French identity than with her Scottish one, perhaps because her memories of these years were more enjoyable than most of her time in Scotland. Compared to the dangers of her first five years, the future did indeed look bright for Mary.

Mary of Guise visited her daughter once in 1550 and returned to Scotland the following year to take on the role of regent in Scotland for Mary, which title she took officially in 1554. She never saw her daughter again, or her son by a previous marriage, and instead had to manage the complexities of English-Scottish-French international politics, as well as manage the factionalism of Scottish domestic politics which was compounded by religious differences between Catholics and, increasingly-vocal, Protestants. The war between England and Scotland had continued and, despite the French presence, it was not until troubles in England forced the Duke of Somerset to return home, followed by the rest of the English troops chased out by a combination of the arrival of further French troops, famine and disease, that peace was agreed. Peace between France and England was negotiated at the Treaty of Boulogne in March 1550, and finally peace between Scotland and England in June 1551. Many French troops left, but those who remained held important positions in the queen mother's household. De Roubay was vice-chancellor and Villemore was comptroller, and the French ambassador, D'Oysel, was very influential. The Scots were weary, and wary, of both French and English interference and after 1554 began to resent the presence of Frenchmen in key positions. Although Mary and her mother did exchange affectionate correspondence, the difficulties faced by Mary of Guise did not hold much interest for her daughter.

During this time, the religious question continued to be an important issue but both Mary of Guise and Archbishop Hamilton – Châtelherault's brother – were more 'tolerant' than Beaton had been and Protestant preachers were not imprisoned or executed. Mary of Guise needed the support of those nobles who expressed pro-Protestant, and possibly pro-English, tendencies in order to ensure that her daughter's marriage to the Dauphin would take place. Edward VI had died in 1553 and was succeeded by his sister Mary, daughter of Henry's first wife Catherine of Aragon, who was Catholic. 'Bloody Mary', as her opponents called her, was determined that her faith should be restored and Protestants were treated harshly during her reign. However, her policies were reversed on the accession of her half-sister Elizabeth, daughter of Anne Boleyn.

In 1557, as negotiations for Mary's marriage to François were under way, several Protestant nobles signed a bond in which they bound themselves to God and declared their intention to overthrow the Catholic church. This First Bond, was signed in December 1557 by the Earls of Glencairn, Argyll, and Morton; Lord Lorne, son of Argyll; and John Erskine of Dun – but it did not attract as much support as was hoped and it would be another two years before the Protestant lords would take a more effective stance.

While Mary's mother was a full participant in Scottish society and politics, Mary herself was not given any preparation for this. Indeed she was not educated in French politics either. Unlike the role forced on her mother, as a female, Mary was not expected to be an independent ruler, but a consort, a subordinate partner, in the marriage to François. Mary was being prepared for her role as future queen of France, and so her position as the current queen of Scots was of less importance to Henri, her French relatives and to Mary herself. She was introduced to her future husband when she joined the household of the French royal children at the Castle of Carrières (Chateau de Carrières) near St Germain. François was quite an unhealthy and fragile child but the young couple appeared to like each other. Henri II also liked his future daughter-in-law; even her future mother-in-law, Catherine de Medici, regarded her quite favourably in the early years. Mary's contact with her Scottish companions was reduced as she spent more time at the royal court. The Valois court was one of the largest and most sophisticated in

16th-century Europe and Mary participated fully in it; travelling from place to place, enjoying riding and hunting; music and dancing; reading and embroidery; eating and drinking; gossiping and scheming. She had, after all, been Henri II's mistress, Diane de Poitiers, protégé.

French and Scottish representatives negotiated the formal wedding contract between 1557 and 1558. Mary took no part in these discussions. Among the Scots commissioners sent to France by Mary of Guise were Lord James Stewart, Mary's half-brother, and Erskine of Dun, both of whom had Protestant sympathies. Because of his own problems with Spain, and potentially England, Henri II was eager to hasten the final uniting of the two countries, but the Scots were still reluctant to acquiesce to all of France's proposals. The Scots wanted assurance about their country's liberties and laws, and were reluctant to acknowledge what might be perceived as France's suzerainty over Scotland: the authority of one sovereign over another sovereign, and thereby one state over another autonomous state – thereby recalling fears of similar attempts at domination by England. As well as national worries, Châtelherault, and his eldest son, James, also wanted to ensure their right of inheritance of the Scottish crown if Mary was to have no children. François was to have the crown matrimonial only while Mary lived. In the event, the crown was never sent to France by the Scottish parliament.

The formal betrothal took place on 11 April 1558 and the official contract appeared to recognise the rights of the Scottish kingdom. There was, however, another secret contract that had been signed at Fontainebleau by Mary without the advice of any of the Scots, although it likely that her

Louvre Palace

Guise relatives may have influenced her decision. In Mary's defence it is quite possible that she did not know that the wording of these documents would not be legal in Scotland. This other contract stated that the Scottish crown would pass to the French if Mary had no children, and that the kingdom of Scotland was to be put up as surety against the cost of her own personal expenses in France, and for any expenses which might be incurred by France in defending Scotland. The fact that four of the Scottish commissioners died before they returned to Scotland – and it would appear that they did not die of natural causes – has given rise to speculation that they may have found out about these secret agreements. The cause of their deaths has never been fully explained.

Mary and François were officially betrothed in the Great Hall of the Louvre Palace in Paris, this event being followed by a lavish ball. The actual ceremony and more celebrations would take place on 24 April 1558. Mary's uncles enjoyed their reflected glory as their niece married the heir to the French throne and a future Valois-Guise-Lorraine royal dynasty became a distinct possibility.

MATRIMONY TO MISERY

The marriage was solemnised on Sunday 24 April 1558. The wedding party proceeded from the Louvre to the Cathedral of Notre Dame, passing through the Paris crowds. In keeping with the marriage customs of the time, the actual wedding vows were taken at the doors of the cathedral, followed by a Mass inside. The city was crowded with the large number of visitors and guests who had travelled to witness the ceremony. The wedding was a time of great merriment and spectacle: music, masques, entertainment, food, scattering of money – poor oots – colour and happiness. The revels continued with a banquet and ball, and the general atmosphere of festivity continued for several months. In Edinburgh the marriage was celebrated with bonfires and processions

Mary went against French custom by wearing a white dress. White was the traditional colour of mourning for the French royal court and brides usually wore silver, gold or purple. Mary was very tall, almost six feet, had auburn hair and a clear skin, and was regarded as quite a beauty. Her dress

Cathedral of Notre Dame

MARY'S FAMILY TREE

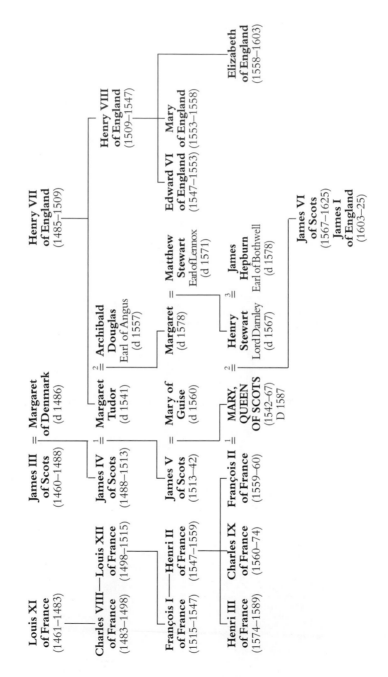

James III of Scots (1460–1488) = Margaret of Denmark (d 1486)

Henry VII of England (1485–1509)

Louis XI of France (1461–1483)

Charles VIII — Louis XII of France of France (1483–1498) (1498–1515)

James IV of Scots (1488–1513) =¹ Margaret Tudor (d 1541) =² Archibald Douglas Earl of Angus (d 1557)

Henry VIII of England (1509–1547)

Edward VI of England (1547–1553)   Mary of England (1553–1558)

Elizabeth of England (1558–1603)

François I — Henri II of France of France (1515–1547) (1547–1559)

James V of Scots (1513–42) = Mary of Guise (d 1560)

Margaret (d 1578) = Matthew Stewart Earl of Lennox (d 1571)

Henri III Charles IX of France of France (1574–1589) (1560–74)

François II of France (1559–60) =¹ MARY, QUEEN OF SCOTS (1542–67) D 1587 =² Henry Stewart Lord Darnley (d 1567) =³ James Hepburn Earl of Bothwell (d 1578)

James VI of Scots (1567–1625) James I of England (1603–25)

complemented her colouring and sparkled with diamonds and jewelled embroidery; she also wore a gold crown covered with diamonds, rubies, sapphires, emeralds and pearls, which was so heavy she could hardly wear it for any length of time. She wrote in a letter to her mother on the morning of the wedding: 'All I can tell you is that I account myself one of the happiest women in the world'.

At the banquet, part of the entertainment was a narration of the legend of Jason and the Argonauts and their quest for the Golden Fleece; Henri II was cast as Jason and by capturing the fleece he would be able to establish an empire. François and Mary were not only the dauphin and queen of France and Scotland, but they would unite the crowns of France, Scotland and England: the empire of Henri's allegory. Indeed Henri II encouraged Mary to press her claim to the English throne and ordered her new coat of arms to include those of England, as well as Scotland and France. When Mary Tudor died on 17 November 1558, Protestant Elizabeth was not recognised as a legitimate queen of England by much of Europe as her father's divorce from Catherine of Aragon was not legal. On her succession, Elizabeth initially attempted a policy of reconciliation by appealing to both Protestants and Catholics. However, many Scots, French, and even English, still preferred Mary Stewart, as a granddaughter of Margaret Tudor and great-granddaughter of Henry VII; Henri II could certainly see there were many political advantages to this plan. However, these claims did little to help develop a positive relationship and would damage later negotiation and communication between the two queens.

The situation in Scotland was still uncertain as the pro-French and pro-English parties fought for control. As regent, Mary of Guise's pro-French policies contributed to the revival of pro-English attitudes among some of the Scottish political elite. Discontent with the Catholic church increased among certain sections of the Scottish population, and found a voice by the end of 1558 and the beginning of 1559. In January the Beggars' Summons was nailed to the doors of friaries throughout the land. It stated that friars should leave, and hand over their goods and monies to the poor. There were economic and political aspects to this document as much as religious ones. Châtelherault, who was by this time openly pro-English, was in communication with the Englishman Sir Henry Percy, as the Scottish Protestants were concerned about the threat of a French Catholic invasion. Following the limited success of the First Bond in 1557, the Protestant lords had continued to agitate for reform. Mary of Guise had directed Archbishop Hamilton, Beaton's successor, to conduct another provincial council to examine the state of the church in Scotland and recommend internal reforms.

The council met in March and in April 1559 the Treaty of Cateau-Cambrésis between France, Spain and England was agreed. Princess Elisabeth de Valois, Mary's sister-in-law, married Philip II of Spain as a result of Cateau-Cambrésis, and there was to be a period of peace in Europe. Henri became less bullish in his support for Mary's claim to the English crown; in contrast, in England, Elizabeth became less tolerant of Catholics. In France, the celebrations to mark the marriage between Elisabeth de Valois and Philip were to prove momentous in more than one way.

In keeping with Renaissance convention, Henri II was very fond of jousting as a way to demonstrate chivalric skill, speed and horsemanship. Several jousting tournaments had been arranged in which he planned to participate. It is claimed that the astrologer Nostradamus told Catherine de Medici of a dream he had had that predicted the death of the king: 'A young lion shall overcome the older one on the field of combat in single battle; He shall pierce his eyes in a golden cage, two forces one, then he shall die a cruel death'. Henri's escutcheon, his heraldic shield, was engraved with a lion. However the claim about the prediction was only made in 1614, many years after the deaths of Henri, Catherine and Nostradamus himself. Clothed in black and white, the colours of his mistress Diane de Poitiers, Henri successfully jousted three times. He then challenged Gabriel de Lorges, (Gabriel Montgomery) Count of Montgomery and captain of the *garde écossais,* to a second bout but on this occasion his opponent's lance broke and a splinter pierced Henri's left eye. Gabriel was absolved of any blame but he was disgraced and later converted to Protestantism. Attended by his close family, but not his mistress, Henri died from his wound ten days later and was buried at St Denis Basilica. François was declared king of France and he and Mary were crowned at Rheims in September 1559. The ceremony was marked by an inauspicious start as, due to a sudden heavy rainstorm, the actual coronation service had to be postponed for a day.

A struggle for power and influence over the young king and queen began. On one side there was François's mother, the powerful Catherine de Medici, on the other, Mary's relatives, the Guises, particularly the Cardinal of Lorraine. François was entirely unsuited to, or perhaps unready for, his regal responsibilities, and showed little interest in affairs of state, preferring to spend time hunting, which he enjoyed with a passion. With the Guises back at the centre of power, they revived their Franco-British imperial plans for Mary. François's advisors attempted to persuade the young king to attend to his duties, but with little success. Catherine began to transfer her attention to her second son, Charles, as the heir to the throne if François and Mary produced no children, and one whom she would be able to control without interference from the Guise faction. Religious strife had also increased in both France and in Scotland. François and Mary found themselves caught in an unenviable position: the freedom and innocence of their childhood had quickly passed.

Religious and political problems had escalated in Scotland as further Scottish nobles, including Lord James Stewart, joined the Protestant cause. After Mary became Queen of France, more French troops had been sent to Scotland and garrisoned at Leith. In October the Protestant lords marched on Edinburgh and proceeded to suspend Mary of Guise from the regency. This provisional government of 24 nobles may have held the capital of the country, but it lacked the money required to administer and further their cause, and by November they had to evacuate to Stirling after an unsuccessful attack on Leith. Mary of Guise re-took Edinburgh but the next couple of months resulted in stalemate as it became clear that neither group would be able to take power without outside help. The Protestants requested help from England and in February 1560 the Treaty of Berwick was signed between Elizabeth of England and the Scottish Protestants, Elizabeth promising to help their rebellion against Mary of Guise and to assist their campaign against the French. William Cecil, Elizabeth's chief advisor, convinced the English Privy Council that Scotland would become an English dependency and so further his long term project of turning the British Isles into a united Protestant country. The English fleet sailed north in order to cut communication between the French based in Leith and the French mainland.

Edinburgh Castle

The siege of Leith started around the end of March 1560 and Mary of Guise moved into Edinburgh Castle as a safer alternative to Holyroodhouse on 1 April. She was not to see the end of the siege, dying of dropsy, an accumulation of body fluids, on 11 June. Her death enabled the hostilities in Scotland to end but it did not necessarily make things easier for her daughter.

The Treaty of Edinburgh was signed on 6 July 1560 as a result of the death of Mary of Guise. Her daughter, Mary, despite being queen had little part to play in the negotiations, which were conducted by the Scottish lords (led by Lord James Stewart,) England (Cecil) and the Guises. Both English and French troops were to be withdrawn from Scotland; François and Mary were to renounce their claim to the English crown and recognize Elizabeth as rightful queen of England. This was a complete reversal of earlier Guise policy. As queen, Mary was to remain as an absentee ruler and the council of nobles was to become the official government. The following month the Scottish parliament accepted a reformed Confession of Faith, rejected papal authority and forbade the practice of the Mass. In order to give authority to their actions François and Mary were to ratify these acts, something that Mary never did.

On hearing about the death of her mother Mary took to her bed for a month in grief. There is a famous portrait of Mary at this time, painted by François Clouet. In it she is depicted wearing a *deuil blanc,* a white hood with a gauze veil, which indicated mourning. However, she had more loss ahead. Rumours had circulated about possible pregnancies from the first night of her marriage; if Mary fell pregnant it would not only ensure the continuation of the Stewart and Valois dynasties, it would increase her security and influence. For a short time in September Mary's appearance suggested she might be pregnant but by the end of the month it was clear she was not. Then, in November, François returned from hunting complaining of a sore ear. Earache was one of his frequent ailments and little was thought of it. After fainting, François developed a fever and was purged and bled by his doctors. His wife and his mother, who fought over the right to see to his needs, nursed him continually. Stories spread that the king was fatally ill or that he had been poisoned. The infection then developed into a brain abscess and he died on 5 December 1560. Mary was now a widow and no longer Queen of France. Her powerful mother-in-law took over the running of the state on behalf of Charles IX, François's younger brother, who was ten years old. Mary's immediate future was uncertain: she had no official place in France.

ADIEU FRANCE; BONJOUR ÉCOSSE

Ce qui m'était plaisant
Ores m'est peine dure
Le jour le plus luisant
M'est nuit noire et obscure;
Et n'est rien si exquis
Qui de moi soit requis

He who was my dearest
Already is my plight
The day that shone the clearest
For me is darkest night.
There is nothing now so fine
That I need make it mine.

(Ode on the death of her husband,
King François II, translation by Robin Bell)

Mary wore the white of mourning that was expected of royalty, and embarked on forty days of isolation from public view. She may have been bereaved about François's death but she was also pragmatic and aware of her uncertain situation. Her relatives urged her to consider potential suitors. Don Carlos, Philip II of Spain's son, was one of their preferred options but the king of Denmark, the king of Sweden, the dukes of Ferrara and Bavaria also all made offers, as did Arran, eldest son of Châtelherault. Marriage to Don Carlos would have been one of dynastic advantage, wealth and honour. The dynastic possibilities, which would have given Spain, one of France's old rivals, a useful ally, were such that Catherine de Medici opposed the match. Spain also had an entente with England, despite Elizabeth's Protestant policies, and did not pursue the plan. By spring 1561 the Spanish match was off and Mary planned to return to Scotland.

The danger, about which her Catholic advisors warned, was that Scotland was now, to all intents and purposes, Protestant, and Mary, as a Catholic monarch, would have difficulties governing unless she managed to drive out the controlling Protestants. But Mary was less concerned about possible dangers, and increasingly aware that Scotland and the Scots were hers by birth. She was conscious that it was her responsibility to govern now that the country lacked any official regent. She appointed men who had

25

some experience of Scotland to her staff, including D'Oysel who had worked for her mother in Scotland. She also took advice from Lord James Stewart who, although Protestant, was not a hard-line supporter of the cause. During her negotiations with Elizabeth's representatives, the Earl of Bedford and Sir Francis Throckmorton, she refused to ratify the Treaty of Edinburgh, noting that she had not been party to its wording or agreement

Although the death of François had posed dynastic problems for Mary, in Scotland the concerns of those governing the country continued to be more about the Protestant settlement and church organization. The Book of Discipline, the statement of reformed church policy, had taken some time to compile, and by January 1561 its acceptance by nobles and lairds was only qualified. The reformed church attempted to establish its organization at parish and higher level, but as a wider system of presbyteries would not appear until later, the supervision of the parishes was to be done by superintendents, often men who had held positions as pre-Reformation bishops. An embryonic form of General Assembly met in December 1560 and April 1562, but the Book of Discipline had not clarified the formal relationship between church and state. It was not clear if the state would have authority over the church or if the church would develop independently from the state.

Opinion in Scotland was also divided, and there were still areas of major disagreement. The possible return of Mary met with mixed responses: those who were still Catholic welcomed the possibility; some Protestants did not. Lord James Stewart was sent to France by the Protestants and proposed that Mary could return to Scotland, and remain faithful to her chosen religion, as long as she did so in private and did not try to further the Catholic cause using foreign support. The Scottish Catholics, led by the Gordon, Earl of Huntly, and John Leslie, a Catholic lawyer, convened at Stirling and drew up an alternative proposal. Leslie, who met Mary in France, advised caution in her dealings with Lord James and suggested that Mary should land at Aberdeen, where she would be met by loyal Catholic men, who would accompany her to Edinburgh and help restore her royal authority, and the Catholic faith.

A third plan came from the seriously disturbed James, Lord Arran. Earlier he had offered a marriage proposal to Elizabeth that had been swiftly rejected. He then turned to Mary, who also dismissed his foolish suggestion. Arran was a staunch Calvinist and supporter of John Knox and one of the extreme Protestants who were vehemently opposed to Mary. He may already have been displaying aspects of his mental instability at this point. In 1562, the following year, when Mary was in Scotland, there were claims that he

Kinneil House

planned to abduct Mary and force her to marry him. His father confined him at the Hamilton property of Kinneil House in Bo'Ness, from where he escaped although he was later recaptured and imprisoned. He inherited his father's title in 1575 but, having been declared insane, he was kept away from politics and cared for by his family.

Mary appeared to welcome the solid advice of her half-brother. She may have been loyal to the Catholic faith, but she was also pragmatic and adaptable, especially when there were few alternatives available to her. She also knew she had to accept Lord James's allies as her advisors: William Maitland of Lethington and James Douglas, Earl of Morton. Mary demonstrated a maturing political awareness by rejecting the offer from Leslie and Huntly, and agreed to a policy of toleration and conciliation, both for Scottish Protestants and for herself. She wanted assurance that she would be allowed to attend Mass and take Catholic communion in private with no interference. However, she continued to delay ratifying the Treaty of Edinburgh.

Mary made preparations to leave France. Travel in foreign lands required guarantees – passports – for safe conduct. As a formality, Mary applied to Elizabeth for safe passage through English waters. Cecil and Elizabeth were not satisfied that Mary had fully ratified the terms of the Treaty of Edinburgh, and so there was a delay after Mary's request was received. Cecil suggested that if Mary renounced her claim to the English crown and ratified the treaty, she might be recognised as Elizabeth's heir. Mary did not accept this offer and she left Paris on the 25 July 1561, bound for Calais accompanied by three Guise-Lorraine uncles, friends, household servants and of course, the Four Marys. By 14 August, although no official safe conduct had been received from Elizabeth, Mary decided that she could no longer hold off her departure, and despite anxieties about possible interceptions by English ships, Mary and her entourage set off into a misty sea.

Against the weather omens, and dodging English ships in the Channel, Mary's convoy made good time and they sailed into Leith harbour at about nine o'clock in the morning of 19 August. Although a summer day, a typical Edinburgh sight welcomed the returning queen: a dense haar rose off the Firth of Forth obscuring any view of the city. Although the Scots knew her arrival was imminent, Mary had arrived sooner than expected and so, as the royal party disembarked, a relatively small crowd of local people and a few officials greeted Mary.

The sight of their queen, dressed in mourning but accompanied by her colourfully-dressed party, posed the local officials with a dilemma of protocol; they had no idea where to take her or what to do with her. No contingency plans had been made, so Lamb's House, the house of a local merchant Andrew Lamb, was requisitioned for her use. There she could rest while messages were sent to Edinburgh. By the afternoon, and after some

Lamb's House, Leith

refreshment, Mary moved to Holyroodhouse, escorted by her hastily gathered nobles. The way was lined with cheering crowds welcoming her home, entranced by the sight of their pretty young queen who herself appeared delighted by the warmth of the welcome from her subjects. If Mary had doubts about her decision to return to Scotland when she first arrived, they were dispersed by this joyous, enthusiastic support.

During her first night at Holyroodhouse the Edinburgh crowds regaled Mary and Alexander Scott composed the poem 'Ane New Yeir Gift' to commemorate her arrival. Things seemed to have progressed smoothly.

> Welcum, illustrat Ladye, and oure Quene;
> Welcum oure lyone, with the 'Fleur-de-lyce';
> Welcum oure thrissill, with the 'Lorane' grene;
> Welcum oure rubent rois upoun the ryce;
> Welcum oure jem and joyful genetryce;
> Welcum oure beill of 'Albion' to beir;
> Welcum oure plesand Princès, maist of pryce;
> God gif ye grace aganis this guid new-yeir
>
> (Alexander Scott, 1561)

RIOTS AND REVELS
MARY'S WELCOME TO PROTESTANT EDINBURGH

Not all of her subjects were taken with Mary or delighted to see her return. In particular John Knox, self-appointed voice of the Reformation in Scotland, feared that her arrival would halt the progress of Protestantism and tempt less determined minds back towards 'idolatry'. The Sunday after her

Palace of Holyroodhouse, former Chapel Royal

arrival in Edinburgh, Mary attended Catholic Mass at the Chapel Royal at Holyroodhouse. A French priest conducted the service and her right to take Catholic communion had been included in the negotiations prior to her return to Scotland. During the service a commotion developed outside led by Patrick Lindsay, son of an ally of John Knox. The crowd demanded the death of the priest but a riot was prevented by the intervention of Lord

James Stewart who persuaded the crowd to disperse. Being a Catholic queen in a Protestant country, albeit Protestant on somewhat dubious legal grounds, was not going to be a straightforward task for Mary. The following day, Mary's first proclamation as active Queen of Scots, was a reassurance that she would not alter the current state of religion in the country; the *status quo* was preserved. This meant the Protestant church was safe from royal interference – Scots could worship as they pleased – but she also maintained she had the right to participate in private Catholic worship. Members of her household also attended Mass, much to the annoyance of Arran who was still active at this time. As with most of Mary's decisions, opinions remain divided about whether she demonstrated pragmatic toleration or a lack of desire to rule with confidence at this point, but what were her options? Impose Catholicism and anti-Protestant legislation as Mary Tudor had done and so increase fear and resentment or maintain a watching brief until a more suitable opportunity arose to capitalise on residual loyalty to the old church?

The formal welcome and triumphant arrival was celebrated on 2 September. Having seen and understood the significance of royal arrivals in France, she was keen to replicate something similar in Scotland involving music, singing, and welcoming allegorical pageants. Mary left Holyroodhouse and re-entered through a special entry in the town wall and rode up to Edinburgh Castle accompanied by key members of the Scottish nobility. The only ones who were absent were Châtelherault and his son, Arran. There a state banquet was served and cannon were fired in celebration from the castle.

After this, she led a procession down Castle Hill (and the Royal Mile) to Holyroodhouse. She was carried in a purple canopy, with a gold fringe, which was met by 50 townsmen disguised as Moors. They were dressed in yellow and wore black hats and masks. When she reached the Lawnmarket, Mary was treated to the first of several pageants organised by the town council that were strongly Protestant in sentiment. There was a painted arch, above which a choir of children sang, and as Mary passed through the arch, a globe opened from where a child, painted in gold to look like an angel, descended. He presented Mary with the symbolic keys to the town and two purple velvet-covered books. One was the Bible, in English, and the other the Protestant psalter. The child also recited some verses of welcome to Mary; all of which gifts and symbols were rather less than subtle in their meaning and support of Calvinist Protestantism.

A play was performed at St Giles with virgin maidens (boys) as the virtues: Fortitude, Justice, Temperance and Prudence. There were further pageants at other locations in the High Street that also had Protestant significance. The performance at the Salt Tron was stopped by the Earl of Huntly, who arrived before Mary and replaced it with an improvised, but less overtly, Protestant, display.

The celebration may not have been as impressive as Mary hoped, as it was clearly an attempt to influence her religious policies rather than celebrate her return. Mary understood the message that was being conveyed; she also understood that the claims that had been made that 'all men' in Scotland were Protestant were exaggerated. There were areas outside Edinburgh where many continued to participate in Catholic worship and even in Edinburgh, Mass had been celebrated openly at Easter. Mary decided to summon John Knox to meet her. She held him responsible for these insults and threats, even though Knox had not participated and had criticised the town council for giving Mary any kind of welcome, insulting or not. He claimed the whole celebration was idolatrous.

Although she indicated that she intended to permit freedom of worship for her Protestant subjects, as a rightful monarch, Mary also had some authority over the spiritual care of her subjects. However, she was also aware that religious unrest could turn to civil unrest, and she was anxious to avoid this possibility. Mary therefore agreed to meet John Knox in the hope that she could have a thoughtful and considerate debate with him. Unfortunately, Mary under-estimated Knox's attitude to women: he did not mind women if they were obedient and Protestant but opposed those who were educated and opinionated, and particularly those who were Catholic. It is well known that she was reduced to tears as a result of their encounters but accounts of their meetings were recorded by Knox and do little to present a balanced view of their discussions and her behaviour.

Knox had been a follower of George Wishart, the Protestant preacher burnt by Cardinal Beaton, and had been involved in the siege of St Andrews Castle, after which he was sent to France as punishment. On his release, he went to England and preached successfully there until the reign of Mary Tudor. Mary Tudor's anti-Protestant campaign forced Knox to flee to Geneva for safety, but he returned to Scotland in 1559 and participated in the campaign to denounce Mary of Guise and Catholicism. Knox's preaching was noted for its vehement oratory and led to riot and iconoclasm, when church carvings and other Catholic icons were destroyed, particularly in Perth. Knox was appointed Protestant minister of Edinburgh on 7 July 1559 but, when it looked as if Mary of Guise might remain as regent, absented himself from the town. He returned to Edinburgh when Mary Queen of Scots arrived and preached a sermon against her being allowed to take Mass.

Their meeting took place in September, shortly after the pageants, in her presence chamber at Holyrood, The interview was not a success, but the ground rules had been set; neither would be willing to change their opinion. Nobility and ambassadors followed court protocol in their meetings with Mary and afforded her the respect she deserved as a queen; Knox did not. Mary immediately addressed Knox's publication *The First Blast of the Trumpet against the Monstrous Regimen of Women,* which had been published in Geneva in 1558. In it Knox stated that female monarchy was repugnant to God and scripture. According to Knox, Mary accused him of all sorts of demonic practices to which he replied with 'simple truth' and 'honest answers'. Mary and Knox engaged in heated debate about God's relationship and authority over monarchs and whether subjects could and should disobey their rulers if it was perceived they acted as tyrants and against God's will. This was tantamount to treason and as such Mary was entitled to be appalled

THE FIRST BLAST.[9]
TO AWAKE WOMEN
degenerate.

O promote a woman to beare rule, superioritie, dominion or empire aboue any realme, nation, or citie, is repugnãt to nature, côtumelie to God, a thing moft contrarious to his reueled will and approued ordinãce, and finallie it is the fubuerfion of good order, of all equitie and iuftice.

In the probation of this propofition, I will not be fo curious, as to gather what foeuer may amplifie, fet furth, or decore the fame, but I am purpofed, euen as I haue fpoken my confcience in moft plaine ãd fewe wordes, fo to ftãd content with a fimple proofe of euerie membre, bringing in for my witneffe Goddes ordinance in nature, his plaine will reueled in his worde, and the mindes of fuch as be mofte auncient amongeft godlie writers.

And firft, where that I affirme the em-

B I

The First Blast of the Trumpet…

by Knox's insolence. Mary was driven to tears after Knox left, not because she behaved like a toddler unable to control her emotions, but more likely through frustration and rage. She had maintained her dignity in the face of what was, to a 16th-century monarch, a heretical and treasonable argument.

Mary may have been unsettled by Knox's clear religious intolerance but she had no intention of embarking on a campaign to enforce Scots to renounce their legally questionable Protestant church. It was clear that in order to survive, Mary had to play a game of reconciliation and compromise. She also had to reassure Catholic powers in Europe that she would carry out her duties as a Catholic monarch. Mary worked with her Protestant nobles, acknowledging that it was better to have them on her side than against her. To this end, she even made it clear that she rejected the counsel and advice of those who had Catholic tendencies. Mary governed the country through her privy council, which was, at this time, mostly Protestant: seven out of the twelve. She attended meetings and listened to the debates of her nobles, contributing to the discussion when needed. On the other hand, Mary's household and private entourage was largely made up of Catholics and those who had accompanied her from France: the Four Marys, musicians, poets, dancers, chefs and physicians. She would listen to the music of David Rizzio and the poetry of Pierre de Chastelard, both of whom were Catholic.

TRAVELS AROUND HER KINGDOM

The royal court did provide some opportunity for the mixing of Mary's Protestant Scottish nobles and her predominantly Catholic household. She commissioned George Buchanan to write masques for the court. These were extravagant entertainments, based on Classical legends, with special stage effects and costumes. Mary enjoyed dressing up and participating in them: it is also claimed she disguised herself as an ordinary woman, and even as a man, and would walk around Edinburgh without being recognised. However, it was not only in disguise that Mary met her subjects. Mary knew that the support and welcome of ordinary Scots was important. Having experienced life at the peripatetic French court, she was aware that moving around a kingdom gave both monarch and subjects opportunities to see each other. Public journeys throughout the country would enable her to display her political strength and govern her subjects, as the privy council could travel with her. Also Mary remembered little of her country of birth and these progresses allowed her to see her realm more fully, as well as removing her from Edinburgh and the irritating John Knox. Between 1562 and 1565 two-thirds of her time was spent on royal progresses; between August 1562 and September 1563 she covered 1200 miles and 460 miles between July and September 1564.

The first progress, between 10 August 1562 and 21 November 1562,

Glamis Castle (see next page)

took Mary to Linlithgow Palace where she had been born. From there she travelled to Stirling, Perth, Coupar Angus, Glamis Castle owned by the Lyon family, Edzell Castle, property of the Lindsays, and Aberdeen. She then progressed to the Earl of Moray's castle at Darnaway in Moray, Inverness, Spynie Palace, which was the property of the Bishop of Moray, Aberdeen again and the Keith Castle at Dunnottar. Next she visited Montrose in Angus, Dundee, made another visit to Stirling and finally back to Edinburgh. She also stayed at the Earl of Atholl's castle at Balvenie in September and Arbroath Abbey, in the Abbot's House, in November of that year. The progress started well, but at Stirling there was an incident reminiscent of Holyrood: as she was hearing Mass at the Chapel Royal, there was a scuffle inside the chapel, which again involved Lord James Stewart. At Perth, although there was a cheering crowd to welcome her, some of the pageants performed were overtly anti-Catholic. This appeared to upset Mary and reportedly caused her to faint. In 1562 Mary also visited Crichton Castle, property of the Hepburns,

Crichton Castle

to attend the wedding of her half-brother Lord James (who had been elevated to Earldom of Moray) to Lady Janet Hepburn.

Part of this progress was to the northeast of Scotland where the Gordon family was very powerful. Here Mary faced the first noble revolt of her reign. George Gordon, 4th Earl of Huntly, was an extremely powerful man in his locality, as well as nationally. He was lieutenant in the north, sheriff of

Aberdeen, owned and administered large areas of land and was known to have Catholic sympathies. Indeed, it was his proposal that Mary land at Aberdeen to start a Catholic administration on her return to Scotland in 1561, which Mary had rejected.

Huntly the 'Cock of the North', had administered and benefited from lands in the earldoms of Moray and Mar until 1562, when Mary decided to grant the titles and lands to Lord James. This would have done little to increase her popularity with the Gordons; however Sir John Gordon, one of Huntly's sons, also had plans to persuade Mary of his suitability as a possible husband – by force if necessary. When Mary reached Inverness, the captain of the town under Huntly's instructions refused her entry. Mary's troops rallied to her side and took the garrison; the captain was then executed in punishment for his insolence.

Huntly and his sons assembled the Gordon forces, intending to block Mary's progress to Aberdeen – or possibly kidnap her. Mary had 3,000 men to Huntly's 1,000 and so was able to pass on unharmed. Huntly was summoned to appear before the privy council to explain his actions, but as he failed to appear he was put to 'the horn' which meant he was declared outlawed and forfeited. Huntly advanced on Aberdeen but Mary's forces, led by Moray (Lord James) and Maitland of Lethington, met up with the Gordons at Corrichie, near Aberdeen, on 28 October 1562. The battle was quick and the Gordon forces completely routed. Prior to the battle, the

Huntly Castle

elderly Huntly was said to have been reluctant to engage in combat, and when he was captured he took a sudden seizure, possibly a stroke, and died before his trial for treason. The Gordons lost much as a result of Corrichie: Sir John was executed following the battle, and Huntly was posthumously convicted of treason and forfeited. The Gordon Castle at Huntly was sacked as part of the punishment. Mary had triumphed, demonstrated her authority to punish disloyalty, and planned further progresses.

No matter what political issues were proving problematic or that there were further reports of Knox's repeated accusations about her Catholic idolatry, Mary was reassured by the obvious pleasure that her subjects expressed when they saw her. Even her approach to managing her councillors seemed to work: they discussed and administered while she listened and did her embroidery. She also continued with her claim to the English crown, in the hope that Elizabeth would name Mary her heir. Meetings between the two queens had been proposed, and even scheduled, but never took place. Mary and Elizabeth exchanged personal letters but these were interpreted and mediated by their respective advisors and ambassadors: Maitland of Lethington for Mary and Thomas Randolph for Elizabeth.

Despite taking action against what might have been perceived as a Catholic plot, Mary still had to appease the reformers. There were several prosecutions for saying Mass, Mary did not give an audience to the Jesuit de Gouda and she did not send Scottish representatives to the meetings of the Council of Trent, the forum for discussion between Rome and the reformers, organized by the Catholic church. There was also the growing speculation, associated with any unmarried monarch, about possible suitors, which occupied not only the Scottish nobility and other European powers, but also Mary herself. The possibility of a match with Don Carlos of Spain was again considered, as without the interference of Catherine de Medici, Mary's own Scottish ambassadors could undertake negotiations. This union would very possibly have destabilised the delicate religious tensions in Scotland and reduced her chances of bring named Protestant Elizabeth's heir. Fortunately Don Carlos was ultimately declared unfit, having fallen down stairs and suffering a brain injury.

1563 was to bring other problems for Mary. A shorter journey to Fife was proposed and she set off on 11 February 1563 to travel to Rossend Castle, near Burntisland. Members of her household accompanied her, amongst them Pierre de Chastelard, a young French poet whose admiration of Mary had turned to infatuation and passion. In an incident at Holyroodhouse, following a masque where the closest members of Mary's court dressed up in clothes of the opposite sex, Chastelard was found by her

Rossend Castle c. 1910

attendants, concealed under the queen's bed. Mary was very upset and angry, and ordered the poet to leave her court. No-one seems to have ensured that he obeyed the queen's orders, and Chastelard was still with the queen's household when it arrived at Burntisland.

In the evening, when Mary retired to her bedchamber, he followed her and forced his way in, to find her being disrobed by two of her Marys. There he made physical advances to her until the Earl of Moray came to her aid. These two episodes were fuel for the fires of rumour- and scandal-mongers, and Chastelard had to be dealt with severely in order to maintain the queen's dignity. After being imprisoned he was tried and executed at St Andrews, where, before he died, he quoted from Ronsard's poem 'Hymn to Death': *Je te salue, heureuse et profitable Mort! Des extremes douleurs medecin et confort…* – Hail, happy and profitable Death Extreme pain physician and comfort… Despite attempts at damage limitation, Knox managed to use these incidents in his continued condemnation of Mary.

There was no doubt that Mary wanted to marry again, but she was aware that whoever was chosen had to be acceptable to more than just herself and her council. Her French relatives, and the Pope, continued to advise her by letter, still hoping for a powerful Catholic union. However there was also Mary's claim as heir to the English crown, which would have an effect on her choice.

Elizabeth had neither married nor named her chosen heir, and in early 1563 asserted her right to veto Mary's choice of husband. Mary sent Maitland of Lethington to negotiate with Elizabeth on her behalf. The stumbling block, as far as Elizabeth was concerned, was that Mary had thus far refused to ratify the Treaty of Edinburgh, which meant that Mary would refrain from calling herself Queen of England. Mary, for her part, used the excuse that she could not ratify any treaty without the consent of her parliament, which of course had not met since she had returned. International discussions continued when Elizabeth played her trump card: the English succession and advised her to marry an Englishman. If Mary married someone of Elizabeth's choice then Elizabeth might agree to name Mary as her heir. Elizabeth suggested Robert Dudley, later created Earl of Leicester, who, it was rumoured, was Elizabeth's lover, as a possible match. Elizabeth saw it as a logical and suitable arrangement: by marrying a Protestant Englishman, Mary would become subordinate to him and as such, subordinate to Elizabeth. Mary rejected this offer swiftly, regarding it as an insult.

On 1 July 1563 Mary set out on another progress, this time to the west, Dumfries and Galloway and the Borders. From Edinburgh she travelled

Drumlanrig Castle (see next page)

to Dunipace, Glasgow, Hamilton, centre of the Hamilton family lands, then to Dumbarton Castle and Inveraray Castle, centre of the Campbell Earl of Argyll, another of her Protestant nobles. She then moved to Dunoon, and Eglinton, stronghold of the Montgomery Earls of Eglinton; Hugh Montgomery, the 3rd earl, was a devout Catholic who remained loyal to Mary throughout her reign. Next, she progressed south along the coast to Ayr and then to Dunure, owned by the Kennedys, Earls of Cassillis, another loyal Catholic family. Travelling further south Mary moved to Ardmillan and Ardstinchar held by the Kennedys of Bargany. The entourage then headed to the Abbey of Glenluce and the Priory of Whithorn, both well-known religious sites or pilgrimage routes. Next stop was Kenmure Castle, owned by the Gordons, Viscounts of Kenmure; St Mary's Isle, and then Dumfries. Moving north, Mary called at Drumlanrig Castle, property of the Douglas family; and Crawfordjohn, owned by the Hamiltons; Couthalley, owned by the Somervilles; then the Cockburn stronghold of Skirling Castle. The next port of call was Neidpath Castle, near Peebles, owned by the Hays. Then Borthwick, south of Edinburgh, followed by Dalhousie held by the Ramsays and Roslin, the property of the Sinclairs of Roslin. The progress ended back in Edinburgh in September 1563 after a visit to Craigmillar Castle just outside the city. It is clear from her itinerary that Mary was careful to show no obvious preference to either Protestant or Catholic families and attempted to balance

Craigmillar Castle, courtyard

41

her favours and presence. Her popularity could only be enhanced by her visibility.

In July 1564, Mary once again set off on her travels. In England Elizabeth and her advisors continued to discuss other possible husbands for Mary. This progress between 21 July and 15 September took Mary to Linlithgow again followed by Perth, Blair Castle, the Earl of Atholl's stronghold; Inverness; Gartly Castle, property of the Barclays; Aberdeen and Dundee. Elizabeth, through the mediation of Randolph, continued to plead for Dudley's case, but it was the appearance at court of another young man, who had been brought up in England, who would ultimately play an important role in the fate of both Mary and Scotland.

MARRIAGE AND DYNASTIC TIES

The marriage to Don Carlos was not officially cancelled until the middle of 1564, and earlier the same year, Elizabeth wrote to Mary requesting that she allow the Earl of Lennox, who had been in exile in England, permission to return to his estates in Scotland. Lennox was a great-great-grandson of James II and therefore had a distant claim to the Scottish crown. He had returned to Scotland in 1542 on the death of James V, supported by Cardinal Beaton, against the incumbent regent, and heir apparent, Arran. He married Margaret Douglas, daughter of Margaret Tudor by her second husband, Archibald Douglas, Earl of Angus, who was James V's half sister. Lennox changed sides to support Henry VIII's invasion. As a result, he fled to England where his son, Henry Stewart, would be raised. Henry, Lord Darnley, therefore had connections to both Scottish and English royal dynasties.

Mary agreed to Elizabeth's request and permitted Lennox to return, much to the chagrin of Châtelherault (formally Arran) and others of the Hamilton network. Mary also proposed a meeting with Elizabeth at Berwick so that they might discuss the progress of the Dudley marriage. Was Mary teasing Elizabeth and playing a game of cat and mouse? Elizabeth quickly attempted to cancel Lennox's repatriation but it was too late. Lennox quickly re-established his place in Scottish elite circles and developed a group of supporters who included the Earls of Atholl and Caithness who were Catholic, but also others such as Lords Seton and Home who were Protestant.

In February 1565 Elizabeth allowed Lennox's son, Lord Darnley, permission to travel north. Elizabeth had decided it would be better if Mary did not marry Dudley, whom she had now concluded she did not want to lose and sent Darnley as a substitute. Darnley was tall and extremely good-looking and would prove to have a devastating impact on Mary and her future. He had been brought up by his mother, Lady Margaret Douglas, at Temple Newsam, near Leeds, to be a fine sportsman, well versed in courtly refinements and hoped, by his mother, to be a possible suitor for Elizabeth.

Darnley arrived in Scotland in the beginning of 1565 and Mary first met him at Wemyss Castle, in Fife, on 16 February during another of her progresses. This journey between 16 January and 24 February 1565 included Falkland; the Balfour Castle at Collairnie near Cupar; Ballinbreich Castle, owned by the Leslies, near Newburgh; Balmerino Abbey, and St Andrews. She then travelled to Struthers, a property owned by the Lindsays of The Byres; followed by Lundin Tower near Lower Largo; Durie, and finally to Wemyss Castle. Before returning to Edinburgh Mary called at Dunfermline, staying at the abbey there. Initially relations between Mary and Darnley were very much those of monarch and subject, and Darnley, having been trained at Elizabeth's court, conducted himself as any courtier should. After a visit to Dunkeld, to visit his father, he re-joined Mary as she returned to Edinburgh from Fife.

Darnley made every effort to charm Mary by dancing and singing, and joining in all the courtly pursuits that Mary so enjoyed. Darnley and David Rizzio also got on very well, which pleased Mary, and Darnley also shared Mary's enjoyment of hunting. It is not clear if Mary was already planning to marry Darnley, but when Elizabeth finally announced that if Mary married Dudley she would forfeit her claim to the English throne, Mary was very upset and felt that she had been used by Elizabeth. Whatever her motives, Mary then turned her attention to Darnley as a possible suitor. A marriage between Mary and Darnley would strengthen Mary's, and that of any children's, claim to the English crown. Aside from his family ties, Darnley was neither a strict Catholic nor staunch Protestant; he attended both forms of service, even attending services at St Giles conducted by Mary's erstwhile *bête noire*, Knox. This religious ambiguity made him a less threatening out-and-out Catholic like Don Carlos. If Elizabeth had substituted Darnley for Dudley, it would seem that she had miscalculated by not anticipating the dynastic consequences.

The Darnley marriage plan ruffled many feathers, particularly those of Moray, who feared that Darnley's dynastic connections would reduce Moray's power and influence over Mary and her kingdom. Privately Elizabeth may have seen this marriage as a better alternative, but that was not her reported public reaction. Neither did other Scottish nobility feel that it was a sensible policy, and after Mary spent some time nursing Darnley through a bout of measles in April 1565, some of her most loyal Protestant nobles, including Moray, Argyll, Châtelherault, Glencairn, Morton and Ruthven, signed a bond agreeing to join together to prevent the marriage. The motives behind the signing of this bond probably had as much to do with distrust of Lennox, and anxiety about his increase in power, as the unsuitability of the marriage.

By May 1565, Moray made his opposition to the match clear to Mary, and Argyll refused to attend the convention that discussed, and eventually agreed to, Mary's wishes. Later that month, Mary promoted Darnley to the Earldom of Ross, and in June, Lord Erskine was raised to the Earldom of Mar. With the loss of support from some of her more senior nobles, Mary attempted to create a second line of defence by granting other titles and elevations.

Mary issued a proclamation in July in reply to a supplication from her subjects, which reiterated that she did not intend to interfere with matters of religion. At the same time she requested a papal dispensation from Rome to permit the marriage to Darnley. Mary and Darnley, as blood relatives, and according to church rules, may have been too closely related. The banns, or proclamations, for their forthcoming marriage were announced before any papal permission had been obtained. The wedding was to take place on Sunday 29 July 1565. During the intervening days, Mary made it clear that the opposition to her choice of husband displeased her greatly. She was full of confidence, and could see no obstacle to the wedding and a new happy, and secure, phase in her life.

Mary, dressed in her *deuil blanc* as a sign of her widowhood, was escorted from her chambers at Holyroodhouse to the private chapel. The wedding vows were exchanged and Darnley placed three rings on the fingers of Mary's right hand. The couple knelt for prayers and were blessed by the priest. Darnley then left his bride to her private Mass. On her return to her apartments, her attendants removed her widow's dress and replaced it with a new, brightly-coloured, gown. The wedding celebrations, although perhaps not as sumptuous as those she had experienced in Paris, were merry and lavish. Eating, drinking, music and dancing were enjoyed by the guests into the wee small hours, and handfuls of gold coins were thrown to the watching crowds.

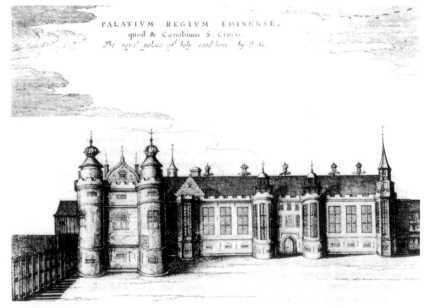

Palace of Holyroodhouse, Jan Goeree e c. 1700

The next day, it was publicly declared that Darnley was to be referred to as King of Scots. Legally Mary was not entitled to grant this and her actions contributed to Darnley's opponents' displeasure. The title did not mean that Darnley was given the crown matrimonial, something that would subsequently irk him as his childish and petulant behaviour became increasingly obvious.

Mary summoned Moray to explain his behaviour and that of others, but he failed to appear. She then declared him 'put to the horn', and officially declared outlaw. This was the start of what was later called the Chaseabout Raid. Moray and the other rebels made for Argyll, and Mary announced that anyone who provided them with aid would be punished. The rebels appealed to Elizabeth for assistance, using the ready excuse of Protestantism as common cause, as well as stressing the dangers associated with Darnley's recent promotion. Whether Mary had found new confidence with her recent marriage, or whether she was actually fearful that the Protestant rebels might succeed is not clear, but she responded with speed and confidence during this crisis. She made it clear that she was not willing to lose all that she had so recently gained, and, summoning her troops, she set out to quash the rebellion, wearing helmet and breastplate to demonstrate her role as a warrior queen. As at Corrichie, Mary showed good leadership when her authority was threatened. She also ordered Edinburgh town council to remove its Protestant provost whom she replaced with Sir Simon Preston of Craigmillar,

Huntingtower Castle, formerly Ruthven Castle (see next page)

who was to prove one of her most loyal supporters in later years.

Mary headed towards Stirling as the rebels, Châtelherault, Moray and approximately 2,000 men, arrived in Edinburgh, but with the change of regime, they found little support there and so made for the southwest and Dumfries. Mary, after a visit to Ruthven Castle, later called Huntingtower, near Perth, returned to Edinburgh where she hoped to raise more support. Having put the rebels to the horn, Mary followed them to Dumfries, ready to resolve the situation by combat if required. By 8 October, Mary and her forces arrived at Dumfries, from where she and Darnley attended a banquet at Lochmaben Castle on 14 October, but Moray had already fled south to try to stir up English support. Elizabeth later refused to grant any of the rebels an audience. It was at Dumfries that Mary met another man, who was later to be an important influence on her: James Hepburn, 4th Earl of Bothwell, a Protestant, who had recently returned from exile. Mary appointed him her lieutenant-general of the Middle Marches when he joined her campaign and credited Bothwell for the successful campaign against the Chaseabout rebels.

The Chaseabout Raid may not have been an auspicious start to her new marriage, but it showed Mary at her most effective and regal: able to respond as the situation demanded, and also able to command a good amount of popular support. The marriage to Darnley may have made some of the Scottish nobility unhappy, but the majority supported her. She returned to Edinburgh and set about the business of governing her kingdom with, she hoped, the support of her husband. The peers of the realm who were now Mary's supporters were: the restored Huntly, Atholl, Lennox and Bothwell; other posts were filled with non-Scots or others of non-noble birth. Mary may have hoped that things would soon settle down; however it soon became clear that Darnley was unsuited for his responsibilities as consort, either because he was too young or because he had other interests. Instead of being a help to Mary, he began to be a hindrance.

TORN BETWEEN TWO HUSBANDS
DARNLEY AND BOTHWELL

Darnley quickly became bored with being Mary's king-consort and did little to support her governing of the kingdom and managing of her political elite. He refused to attend important meetings and criticised Mary for appearing to spend too much time being queen and not enough time with him. His childish behaviour was not only troublesome to Mary, but provided her enemies with ammunition to use against her about her own unfitness to reign. Darnley was resentful that Mary did not grant him the crown matrimonial, something that was not in Mary's power to do. He wanted to be king and as such have Mary, as a female, his subordinate. He was unfaithful to Mary and had several lovers, both female and male, probably including David Rizzio.

Somewhat more dangerously, he dabbled in international affairs between Spain, France and England in support of a Catholic revival. This was dangerous for Mary, as she had tried to maintain a neutral position regarding restoring the Catholic church. In February 1566, after some dodgy dealings, Darnley was to be invested with the French Order of St Michael, which would give him international prestige. There was to be a Catholic Mass prior to the ceremony but the Protestant nobles refused to go, much to Darnley's annoyance.

In an attempt to pacify Darnley, Mary tried to persuade them to attend. Darnley further exacerbated the situation and stated he intended to restore the Mass to St Giles. This incident put Mary in an awkward position: her compromise with the Protestants had not impressed her Catholic supporters in either Scotland or in Europe; and she had not made any attempt to reinstate Catholic worship for her ordinary subjects, which disappointed some.

However, in Mary's defence, she had other issues to consider: she was pregnant. Mary was in the early stages of pregnancy after the Chaseabout Raid and an episode of illness had given rise to rumours, but it was not until she chose to travel back to Edinburgh by carriage, rather than her customary horseback, that the rumour became official; a legitimate heir to the crown of Scotland would be a great boost to morale. The news of her pregnancy pleased some but had the opposite impact on others. It was a pointed message to Elizabeth in England who was unmarried and received the news with dismay. The Hamiltons were also less than pleased: a legitimate and living child would reduce their place in the succession. The fact that Mary and Darnley were increasingly distant was not important to Mary, but would prove to be dangerous.

Darnley became progressively jealous and resentful and the situation was complicated by Mary's intention to forfeit those involved in Chaseabout, apart from Châtelherault, who had already been pardoned. Mary had considered pardoning the rebels, but she changed her mind. Neither the rest of the Protestant, nor even the Catholic, nobles supported Mary's proposal; they were apprehensive that this might set a precedent for further forfeitures. Darnley's father, Lennox, developed a scheme with Argyll to contact Moray and offer him a full pardon if he and the other exiled nobles would agree to give the crown matrimonial to Darnley on their return. This in turn would reduce Mary's power. A bond was drawn up although, cleverly, two of the main conspirators, Moray and Maitland of Lethington, did not sign it. However, there had to be a scapegoat who could be blamed for Darnley's recent apparent support for Catholicism. David Rizzio ticked the boxes: he was Catholic, he was Italian, he was close to Mary, and had replaced Maitland as her secretary. Now he could be cast as a papal spy as well. His convenient murder would embarrass Mary and help all those involved. In England, Cecil and Elizabeth were made aware of the plan.

On the evening of Saturday 9 March 1566, two days after the session of parliament where it was decided that the rebels were to be summoned, David Rizzio was murdered in front of the heavily-pregnant Mary. Mary had been dining in her rooms at Holyroodhouse with her half-sister Jean,

Palace of Holyroodhouse 1908

Countess of Argyll, her half-brother Robert Stewart, and others of her close entourage, including Rizzio. Darnley appeared from his apartments, followed some minutes later by Patrick, 3rd Lord Ruthven, dressed rather surprisingly in full armour. Ruthven, who was very ill and would die some weeks later, announced that he had come for Rizzio. Mary's reaction was to protect herself and her staff; Rizzio tried to hide while Mary's other attendants attempted to restrain Ruthven. As he pulled out a pistol, Morton's men burst into the room and dragged Rizzio down the stairs where he was stabbed as many as 56 times. His body was discarded over a chest; later, a porter stole his clothes. Darnley's dagger was left in the corpse, as evidence of his involvement, as, true to form, at the last moment he had refused to participate in the murder. Rizzio was buried in Canongate cemetery, near Holyroodhouse.

It is possible that Mary may have also been a target but what is more likely is that she might have miscarried as a result of witnessing such a horrific event. This latter possibility might well have suited Darnley's immature character. The following morning, he came to her full of contrition; Darnley was the father of her child and to ensure its legitimacy she had to stand by him, at least in the short term. However, more seriously, Mary had to face yet another political crisis and threat to her, and her unborn child's, royal authority and security. It seemed there was large-scale opposition to her rule. She appealed to Bothwell and Huntly, in the hope that they would provide support. Mary also isolated Darnley from the conspirators. In the early hours of 12 March, only three days after Rizzio's murder, Mary and Darnley left Holyroodhouse, slipping out through back corridors and storerooms. They eventually arrived at Dunbar Castle where Bothwell awaited them; Huntly, Atholl and others joined them later. In order to ameliorate the political fall-out, Mary pardoned the Chaseabout rebels but not those involved in the murder of Rizzio. This left the way free for Moray to return to Scotland and political life without fear of prosecution, as his name was not officially included on the Rizzio bond. Morton and Ruthven went south to England; Maitland of Lethington went north. On her return to Edinburgh on 18 March, once again the conquering heroine, Mary officially accepted Moray, Glencairn and Argyll back into her council.

For her personal safety, Mary moved into Edinburgh Castle where she awaited the birth of her baby; Darnley returned to his life of hedonism, and the relationship between Mary and her husband continued to deteriorate. Prince James was born on 19 June; he was a healthy baby, born with the lucky caul (a piece of amniotic sac) over his head. According to folklore James could, at least, be reassured that he would not die by drowning. Scotland

St Margaret's Chapel, Edinburgh Castle

had a male heir and there was widespread rejoicing and relief; the castle guns were fired in salute, hundreds of celebratory bonfires burned throughout the land, and a service of thanksgiving was held at St Giles. In England, there was also some increased support for Mary, although Elizabeth received the news with less pleasure. 'The Queen of Scotland is lighter of a fair son and I am but barren stock' was her much quoted remark, and the arrival of James meant that he was not only heir to the Scottish throne, but potentially also to that of England. This may have been Mary's ultimate moment of glory, producing a live male child, but ironically it also marked the start of another problem. The male child could offer her opponents a new option as a king of Scots, demoting the position of his mother, the queen.

James was given for safekeeping to the Earl of Mar at Stirling Castle; Mary hoped this would protect the young prince from threats of kidnap, possibly by his Lennox relatives. Meanwhile, she turned to Bothwell for comfort and encouragement. James Hepburn, 4th Earl of Bothwell, was six years older than Mary, and, in contrast to Darnley's tall and elegant good looks, was a short, squat Scotsman. Also, in contrast to Darnley's, and also François's, rather effete personality, Bothwell was physically and mentally strong; he also had a temper which would erupt violently at times, although this side of his personality was not obvious to Mary at first. Although married to Jean Gordon, he had many mistresses. His military strengths and political reliability were important when he was appointed lieutenant-general, however, when Mary became physically and emotionally attracted to Bothwell, it was to be one of her greatest misjudgements.

Although her health was quite fragile after the birth, Mary went on a hunting trip with Darnley to Traquair House, outside Peebles, in August,

Traquair House

and in October she left on a progress to the Borders, holding justice courts. She travelled to Jedburgh where she heard that Bothwell had received an injury during a skirmish with Wee Jock Elliot of Park, a Border reiver.

According to George Buchanan's later account, which is highly critical of Mary, she immediately left Jedburgh to ride to Hermitage Castle where Bothwell lay seriously injured. However, as Mary herself was not feeling very well, it was five or six days before she made the journey, on 15 October. The 50-mile round trip by horse to Hermitage and back, precipitated one of Mary's most serious bouts of illness, during which it was feared she would die. She lay virtually unconscious for at least a week at a tower house, now called Mary Queen of Scots House, in Jedburgh. Treatments prescribed by her French physicians saved her life; her big toes were bandaged, as were her legs from the ankles up and also her arms. Wine was forced into her mouth; she was given enemas and medicinal draughts, after which she vomited up a large amount of old blood.

Although almost moribund, Mary managed to make it clear to those who attended her that Darnley was not to be allowed to take control of either prince James or claim the crown. Mary even wrote to Elizabeth

Mary Queen of Scots House, Jedburgh

requesting that Elizabeth would become James's protector if she died.

Bothwell, and Darnley, who arrived in a foul temper and stayed only a few hours, visited Mary as she recovered. She then continued north via Kelso; Hume Castle, property of the Homes; then to Langton Castle owned by the Cockburns; and Wedderburn another Home stronghold. Mary then stopped at Eyemouth, Dunbar, and then Tantallon Castle, just outside North Berwick, which was at that time still a property of the Douglases. Before returning to Edinburgh, Mary stayed at Craigmillar Castle, Preston of Craigmillar's castle, and it was here that Mary and her privy council appear to have spent many hours in discussion about the problems posed by Darnley.

Darnley was not just Mary's problem: his repeated demands for the crown matrimonial and the title of king, as well as his capricious campaign to reinstate Catholic Mass in Scotland, had made him a political embarrassment for everyone, except the Lennoxes. The likelihood of any reconciliation between Mary and Darnley seemed unlikely. One option, proposed by Maitland of Lethington, was to apply to Rome for an annulment, but as Mary had already applied for special permission to marry in the first place this was not feasible: this would also make her son illegitimate which

Great Hall, Craigmillar Castle

she certainly did not want. Another possible solution was a divorce but this again would impact on the legitimacy of her son. A third suggestion, which Mary rejected, was that Darnley could be disposed of quickly and conveniently by other means, including a charge of treason. No decision was reached formally at this time, but it later became clear that Mary's council had decided on their course of action, which she may not have sanctioned officially. At the same time, Mary was in delicate negotiations with Elizabeth regarding Mary being named Elizabeth's heir apparent and she would not have wanted to do anything that would interfere with this offer.

The baptism of Prince James at Stirling on 17 December was an important ceremony, which had been delayed because of Mary's illness. The event was planned to be a great three-day celebration, reminiscent of the French festivities that Mary had experienced during her childhood. It would be a chance to relax and have pleasure after the strains of the last few months. This was the only time Mary requested a taxation of her subjects as the cost exceeded the personal pension that she received from her French relatives. The celebrations included banquets, masques, mock sieges and fireworks. It was to be a public display of Mary's success and also a chance to demonstrate unity and reconciliation among her nobility: the Chaseabout incident and Rizzio's murder were in the past; even Morton was pardoned as a result of Cecil's petition. However the united front would not last.

The ceremony was to be performed by Catholic rites, conducted by Archbishop Hamilton, and James's godparents were to be the King of France, the Duke of Savoy, and Elizabeth of England. Elizabeth did not attend but she sent a highly-decorated gold christening font as a gift. The King of France's representative, the Count of Brienne, carried the baby to the Chapel Royal, accompanied by Scottish Catholic nobles. Elizabeth's representative, the Earl of Bedford, refused to enter the chapel as he was a Protestant, and he waited outside with Scottish Protestant nobles including the Moray, Huntly and Bothwell. Darnley, despite his apparent Catholic sympathies, did not attend; there was to be no reconciliation with him. Bothwell, now clearly Mary's favourite, stood behind the queen at the banquets, acting as her protector in his new suit of blue which she had provided. Mary also gave Moray a green outfit and Argyll a red one.

Darnley stayed in Glasgow where he was prescribed mercury salivation – the standard treatment for syphilis. Mary spent some time at Drummond Castle near Crieff and in January 1567, she left to visit her sick husband, escorted by the ever-present Bothwell, and also Huntly. After several days

Drummond Castle

55

and several visits, Mary persuaded Darnley to return with her to Edinburgh, where she could keep a close eye on his activities and contacts. Darnley was not happy about returning, as the Rizzio conspirators still blamed him for his cowardice, but he finally agreed and they arrived in Edinburgh on 1 February. He refused to go to Craigmillar, but it was also inadvisable for him to return to Holyroodhouse with Mary until he was fully recovered. He selected Kirk o' Field, a house near Holyroodhouse, as a temporary residence. During the time he spent at Kirk o' Field, meetings between Mary and Darnley were very cordial; she even agreed to sleep in the room below his. However, relations between Darnley and Mary's nobles remained strained. As his health improved it was planned that he would move back to Holyroodhouse but during the early hours of 10 February, Darnley's plans were permanently altered.

On Sunday 9 February there had been a celebration at Holyroodhouse for the marriage of two of Mary's staff, however the queen spent some time in the evening with her husband. It appears the visit was so enjoyable that Darnley wanted Mary to stay the night, but she refused as she had promised to attend the wedding masque. At about two o'clock in the morning of Monday 10 February a large explosion disturbed the town and all that remained of the house at Kirk o' Field was rubble. Darnley and his servant, William Taylor, were found dead in the garden of the house, showing no signs of any injuries caused by an explosion. Darnley and his servant were in their nightshirts and appeared to have been suffocated. The bodies of some servants were found under the rubble, although others survived the blast. Darnley was buried at Holyrood Abbey. Yet again Mary was faced with a crisis of potentially enormous proportions. Would it be revealed that she had conspired in the murder? Or would it be claimed that, as Mary had planned to be in the house at the time, she was therefore also a possible target of the plot?

ASSASSINATION TO ABDUCTION

The murder of Darnley was a shocking event and was never fully explained. Certainly one of the main suspects was Bothwell but others were also involved, including Moray, Maitland of Lethington and Morton. Cecil also appears to have been aware of the intention, if not the detail. The discussions at Craigmillar were certainly linked to the murder but it does appear that there was more than one conspiracy, although whether they were all planned for the same night or mere coincidence is open to conjecture.

Mary appeared terrified that she had also been targeted and immediately moved to Edinburgh Castle for safety; later she went to Seton Castle, in East Lothian. She then issued a proclamation offering a £2,000 reward for any information about those involved. A free pardon was also offered to the first person to confess and inform on the rest of the conspirators; there was no response to either offer. Rumours about Bothwell's involvement circulated and placards were posted which blatantly accused him of the crime. Mary came to Bothwell's defence and she continued to turn to him for advice. More importantly, she refused to agree to any trial. There had been shock and surprise in Paris, and her Guise relatives and Catherine de Medici urged her to avenge the murder or risk damaging her reputation. Elizabeth also advised Mary to summon Bothwell to trial.

With Mary's clear support, Bothwell continued to expand his influence and power; indeed Mary increased his military authority. Their increasing personal closeness gave rise to more rumours that the queen and Bothwell were also physically intimate. Further placards appeared linking Mary and Bothwell. The images were those of a hare surrounded by a circle of swords and the letters JH, for James Hepburn. Bothwell's family crest included a hare and the swords implied he was a murderer. Above the hare was a naked mermaid carrying sexual symbols and wearing a crown, identified by MR. The image of a mermaid symbolised a prostitute, but the addition of a crown and Maria Regina made the insult even clearer.

It was Darnley's father, the Earl of Lennox, who openly accused Bothwell of murder, and the privy council set a trial date of 12 April. However, Bothwell managed to fill Edinburgh with so many of his own supporters that Lennox was afraid to come to the city. The 'trial' was held at the tolbooth but, with Lennox absent, the prosecution had no witnesses or case, and so Bothwell was acquitted. On 19 April Mary attended parliament and formally took the Protestant church under her protection. She also ratified gifts to Maitland of Lethington, Morton, Moray, Huntly and Bothwell. These gifts may have been attempts to ensure continued backing from the most powerful nobles in the country. However, Bothwell also arranged support his own way. That night he invited the nobles to Ainslie's Tavern where he circulated a bond that confirmed he was innocent of Darnley's murder but also that the signatories would support his ambition to marry Mary. There were 29 signatories to the bond, including Morton and Huntly. Did the nobles hope the plan would ruin both Mary and Bothwell? Mary herself appears to have refused Bothwell's proposal several times, perhaps because she anticipated the consequences. Also before any wedding could be officially sanctioned, there was the minor detail of Bothwell's present wife. However, Bothwell's confidence and dominance was such he seemed arrogantly convinced that he would marry Mary.

Mary went to Stirling for a short visit to her son in April and planned to return to Edinburgh via Linlithgow. It was on this journey that Bothwell and his forces intercepted the royal party, which then travelled to Dunbar, where Mary was allegedly raped. Bothwell's wife was persuaded to lodge a petition for divorce, which was issued on 3 May. Mary may have colluded or have been forced to go to Dunbar, opinions were varied, but it seems unlikely that she would not have been released or escaped at some point over the next 12 days if she had commanded it. On 6 May, after staying at Hailes Castle in East Lothian, Mary and Bothwell returned to Edinburgh, to a less

Hailes Castle

than rousing welcome. James Craig, assistant minister at St Giles, refused to read the wedding banns, much to Bothwell's displeasure.

Bothwell was created Duke of Orkney and Lord of Shetland, in order that his status was sufficiently high for him to marry the queen. The wedding contract was signed on 14 May and the ceremony took place the next day. Several features denoted this day as very different to Mary's previous two weddings. 'Marry in May and rue the day' is a popular Scottish saying and for Mary this would turn out to be particularly apt. The wedding took place at 10 o'clock in the morning and, hypocritically, Adam Bothwell, Bishop of Orkney, a relative of Bothwell, conducted the service according to Protestant rites. Mary wore her tradition *deuil blanc* and a highly-decorated black velvet gown. There were few witnesses; most refused to attend. There were no triumphant banquets or masques as this was no celebration or joyous event. The rest of European royalty looked on aghast at Mary's conduct and would do little to support Mary as the situation deteriorated.

THE BEGINNING OF THE END

As Bothwell and Mary started their brief but eventful married life, Bothwell's opponents congregated at Stirling, styling themselves the Confederate Lords. Bothwell's arrogance and cruelty were now quite apparent, and the political repercussions escalated very quickly. He wrote presumptive and over-confident letters to Elizabeth and Cecil, hoping for their support. The Confederate Lords marched from Stirling to Borthwick Castle where the

Borthwick Castle

royal couple were in residence. Mary had relatively few guards but the defences protected them from any serious attack. The Lords took control of Edinburgh where they issued a statement that named Bothwell as both Darnley's murderer and abuser of the queen's authority. Bothwell had already fled Borthwick, and Mary escaped later, disguised as a man. At Dunbar, she issued a proclamation ordering her loyal forces to muster at Carberry Hill, near Musselburgh, from where she would lead the advance to retake Edinburgh. Huntly and Crawford led the Queen's men, and her banner showed the Saltire and the Lion Rampant. Morton and Atholl led the Lords, whose banner was a picture of Darnley's half-dressed body under a tree. The King's men were fighting not just for the future King James, they claimed, but also to revenge Darnley's murder – in which many of them, along with Bothwell, had actually been involved.

The two armies met on 15 June, and much of the day was spent in stalemate, as each side was reluctant to start the attack. Bothwell, in his usual rash manner, was all for single combat, reminding the Lords of their complicity in the Ainslie Tavern bond. Mary tearfully refused to let him fight, stating that the problem was hers. Conflicting reports stated that Mary then offered to break off from Bothwell and surrender herself to the Lords if they promised her safety. Other versions reported that she ordered Bothwell to lead the charge. In the event, Mary's army did not charge and she surrendered to the Lords having arranged for Bothwell to escape.

Instead of being allowed to return to Holyroodhouse, as she had anticipated, the Lords took her to the Lord Provost's house, where she was kept under guard. The Edinburgh crowds jeered and booed as she arrived in the town. From here the increasingly dishevelled queen was taken to the Douglas castle of Lochleven, owned by Sir William Douglas. Morton signed

Lochleven Castle

the warrant for Mary's imprisonment and the Douglases were appointed her custodians. At the castle she fell into a state of collapse and suffered a miscarriage around 23 July. Meanwhile the Lords got to work collating the case against her and appointed George Buchanan to compose their version of events. Buchanan, although Protestant, had been employed in Mary's household and was the author of the many masques and entertainments performed at her court. Buchanan repaid his erstwhile employer by claiming Bothwell and Mary had been lovers for months before Darnley's death, that they had jointly planned the explosion, and that the alleged rape was staged. The Lords were revisionists and shifted all the blame for a crime in which they were involved onto Mary. Mary's detailed version of events, although reported by her ambassadors, was ignored.

The Lords chose to confront Mary while she was clearly in a weak and vulnerable condition just after her miscarriage. On 24 July 1567, Mary agreed to abdicate in favour of her son. She had initially refused to sign or agree to a divorce from Bothwell, but the Lords were anxious to get Mary to sign an agreement, otherwise their actions might be perceived as a rebellion against a rightful monarch. They needed to establish a stable government to restore calm in the kingdom. If the Confederate Lords could not establish a legal government quickly, Mary might be given foreign help. As things stood Elizabeth, the Lords most likely ally, was extremely angry that a legitimate monarch had been treated so badly by her subjects.

There has been much conjecture about how many months pregnant Mary was when she miscarried, calculating that the date of conception might have been before the Bothwell marriage. These questions can never be answered, but Mary was certainly ill, miscarriage or not, in July. Her weakened state probably contributed to her acceptance of the terms offered. She agreed to resign her crown to her son because she could no longer carry out her duties as queen; Moray was to be appointed regent in James's minority but Morton and the Confederate Lords would govern the country until he returned. James was crowned at Stirling Castle, where John Knox preached the sermon and Morton and Lord Home took the oath on James's behalf.

In the meantime Bothwell had attempted to rally troops in support of Mary, but met with little success, even in the northeast stronghold of the Gordons. He then sailed to Orkney and Shetland, where he managed to commission a number of pirate ships. When Kirkcaldy of Grange sailed north with armed ships, Bothwell retreated further north to Norway, where he was eventually imprisoned. For a time King Frederick of Denmark detained Bothwell in the hope that he might be able to obtain the Northern Isles in return for his hostage, but by 1573 Bothwell was imprisoned at

Dragsholm, where he eventually went insane and died in 1578.

As the newly appointed regent, but not king, Moray attempted to establish control over the country. The religious acts of 1560 were ratified, much to the satisfaction of the church. Politically, Moray re-took Dunbar and Edinburgh and restored peace in the Border areas. However, despite all his efforts the country was not united. The Hamiltons and George Gordon, the restored 5th Earl of Huntly, remained loyal to the queen. Mary still had a good amount of ground support that was stirred into action by her dramatic escape from Lochleven.

Two young Douglas males, George and Willie, became so besotted by Mary they helped her escape. They obtained the keys of the castle, and on their second attempt, Mary crept into a boat on 2 May 1568 and was rowed to the shore where horses were waiting. She then met up with Lord Seton and rode to Niddry Castle near Winchburgh. From here she made her way west, to Cadzow Castle, home of the Hamiltons, where she was pledged support from earls, bishops and lords: an alliance of Catholics and Protestants. Her force rapidly increased to 5000 or 6000 men and Mary and her supporters were confident of success and urged her to take action swiftly rather than wait. The King's party had been caught off guard by Mary's escape. Moray was in Glasgow with a relatively small force and Mary ordered her men to march towards Dumbarton to attack before he got reinforcements. Mary may have spent the night before the battle at Craignethan Castle, a Hamilton property. On 13 May the two armies met at Langside, but despite

Craignethan Castle

Battle of Langside Monument c.1900

being outnumbered, Moray's troops were more experienced and outmanoeuvred the Queen's troops. Personality clashes among her supporters weakened their leadership and Argyll collapsed suffering from acute stomach pains.

Mary fled the battlefield and made for Terregles Castle, a Maxwell

Dundrennan Abbey (see next page)

property, and then Dundrennan Abbey in Galloway. It appears that she decided to ask for help from Elizabeth at some point; as another woman and queen, Mary may have hoped that Elizabeth would understand her particular position. She wrote a personal letter and enclosed a ring that Elizabeth had sent her in 1563, as a token of love and friendship. Perhaps more sensibly, however, Mary's advisors thought she should seek help from France, her own, and Scotland's, traditional ally. A message was sent to Sir Richard Lowther, deputy-governor of Carlisle, asking for safe passage for Mary and her party. Without waiting for confirmation of her safe passage from Elizabeth, Mary, disguised as an ordinary woman, boarded a fishing boat on 16 May, a fortnight after her escape from Lochleven. It is possible the boat's destination was France not England, but history records that she spent her first night in England at Workington Hall which was owned by Sir Henry Curwen, a friend of Lord Herries, one of her loyal supporters. Curwen may have invited her, as a royal guest, to shelter at Workington, which certainly provided a safe haven from her Scottish enemies but with hindsight Mary should perhaps have listened to her advisors and continued her journey to France.

HOW DO WE SOLVE A PROBLEM LIKE MARY?
TRIALS AND TRIBULATIONS

Elizabeth was presented with something of a constitutional dilemma when Mary arrived in England. Mary had never officially renounced her claim to the English crown, which displeased Elizabeth, but equally Elizabeth could not be seen to give support to the rebels by holding another monarch in confinement, as this might precipitate French involvement. On balance, Elizabeth was quite sympathetic to Mary at this point; Cecil on the other hand was not. He anticipated that Mary would be a threat to Elizabeth and provide a focus for discontented English Catholics.

Sir Richard Lowther escorted Mary to Carlisle Castle; not straight to London to see Elizabeth as Mary had hoped. Nevertheless she accepted this, and did not realize that Elizabeth had issued instructions to guard Mary closely, not only for her own protection. Mary was allowed members of her household to join her at Carlisle, but as time passed her impatience increased and she wrote numerous letters of complaint to Elizabeth and Cecil and to France. She need not have worried on that latter account, as Catherine de Medici's letter to Elizabeth implied that she was glad not to be involved in Mary's problems. It was not clear to Mary whether she was a royal guest or a prisoner but there were further restrictions on her movements, visitors and communications. Sir Francis Knollys and Lord Scrope were sent north by Elizabeth as emissaries to explain Elizabeth's position and her concerns about Darnley's murder. Scrope was to be Mary's custodian, and Knollys her guardian.

Elizabeth decided that she would order an inquiry into the events surrounding Darnley's death, the Bothwell marriage, Mary's abdication and Moray's role. If Moray was to blame rather than Mary, Elizabeth would help restore Mary but she had to renounce her claim to English throne and her Catholic faith. Mary agreed to this offer, believing that she would be found innocent of all charges. Cecil asked the Lords to provide him with evidence and proof of Mary's complicity, and George Buchanan was again chosen to compile the dodgy dossier, otherwise known as the Casket Letters, which was sent to Cecil in June. On 15 July Mary arrived at Bolton Castle, in Yorkshire, property of Lord Scrope. Bolton was a more secure castle than Carlisle and also meant that Mary was further away from any potential rescue

Bolton Castle, Mary's bedchamber

party from Scotland, where she continued to have support throughout her captivity. It was, however, an ever-decreasing cause that lost momentum, and its figurehead, when Mary fled south. While she was at Bolton she received boxes of her clothes and belongings from Lochleven and also gifts from others, including George Bowes, the Earl of Northumberland. She also received news from Scotland that suggested Moray was unpopular as a regent and that Huntly and Argyll still planned to overthrow the Confederate Lords.

Although Mary was optimistic that the inquiry at York would find in her favour, she was bitterly disappointed that she would not be allowed to attend in person. In October, Scottish and English commissioners met and the Casket Letters were handed over to the Duke of Norfolk. These were purported to be letters and poems exchanged between Mary and Bothwell, showing that they were lovers before Darnley was killed. These letters disappeared soon after the second inquiry at Westminster, but their authenticity has always been doubtful, especially as those who discovered (or doctored) them had so much to gain from anything that blackened Mary's name. Some of them are genuine letters from Mary, some were to Bothwell, and others were not. Some were likely complete forgeries, but Moray, Morton and Buchanan, and Cecil, who also saw and made copies, were able to use them to add weight to their case. The casket that was supposed to have held the letters is now kept at Lennoxlove in East Lothian.

The letters were not used at York; Moray preferred to delay producing them publicly, although the English commissioners had seen them privately. They were not presented to Mary's representatives who insisted, if they were presented as official evidence, Mary would demand to attend in order to deny their authenticity. At the same time, Maitland of Lethington and John Leslie, Bishop of Ross, approached the Duke of Norfolk with a proposal that he might marry Mary, which would make her a duchess and inferior to Elizabeth. The York inquiry was adjourned and reconvened in November at Westminster. Mary had been found neither guilty nor innocent, but there was sufficient doubt about her actions. This was enough to allow Elizabeth to continue to hold Mary in captivity.

The second larger commission resumed at Westminster but was moved to Hampton Court to avoid an outbreak of plague. This time there was much discussion of the Craigmillar bond; Maitland of Lethington was named but denied he was present. Cecil charged Mary formally of complicity in Darnley's death. Mary was dismayed; she and her representatives had been assured this was an inquiry, not a trial. On 6 December the Casket Letters were presented by Moray. There was never a formal verdict given by the second inquiry but in January 1569 Elizabeth proclaimed Mary had not answered the accusation of murdering her husband. Further, Elizabeth recognised Moray as regent in Scotland. Mary wrote to Elizabeth expressing her innocence, pointing out that the letters were forgeries and requesting a

Sheffield Manor Lodge (see next page)

personal audience. Mary was to be moved to Tutbury, without free access and communication and a reduced entourage; George Talbot, Earl of Shrewsbury, and Bess of Hardwick, his wife, were appointed to be her custodians, which responsibility they held for the next 15 years at much personal expense and loss.

The journey to Tutbury was complicated; the medieval castle was in a poor condition and part of its roof was missing. Shrewsbury and Bess had to move furnishings from Sheffield in order to make it habitable. Mary stayed for a short time at Sheffield while Tutbury was prepared for her. Mary hated Tutbury to where she was returned in 1584. In April Mary was moved to Wingfield, which was also quite basic accommodation for a queen, albeit one who had lost her kingdom. Over the next two years Mary was moved between Chatsworth, Wingfield, Manor Lodge at Sheffield, and Tutbury so that the houses could be cleaned or 'sweetened' with fresh rushes and the drains cleared. Shrewsbury, a Protestant, was Bess's fourth husband. Bess of Hardwick was a woman of ambition and wealth, inherited on the deaths of her previous husbands; Chatsworth House was built for her. Although they spent many hours and years in each other's company, not surprisingly Mary and Bess did not like each other. Mary resented Bess's control over her movements and Bess resented both the cost of providing accommodation for Mary and her staff and also Mary's influence over her husband.

In November 1569 Catholic northern nobles, the Earls of Westmoreland and Northumberland restored the Catholic Mass and marched

Wingfield Manor

south; the Duke of Norfolk, who was still in the running as a possible husband for Mary, was also involved. John Leslie, Bishop of Ross, urged them to free the captive queen. As a result, Elizabeth ordered that Mary be moved south to Coventry, where the castle was quite ruinous. Accommodation was provided for a couple of months at the Black Bull Inn and St Mary's Guildhall, during the Northern Rising, which Elizabeth's forces defeated within six weeks. Norfolk was sent to the Tower of London, where Mary wrote him affectionate letters regarding their 'engagement'. On this occasion Norfolk was released from captivity.

MEANWHILE IN SCOTLAND

Mary's cause was not entirely lost and would not be until 1573; several nobles never joined the King's party, particularly Huntly and Châtelherault. The two parties were not divided simply along religious lines; although the King's party supported the Protestant church, there were both Catholics and Protestants on Mary's side. Often the division occurred along political and dynastic rivalries. The northeast was held for Mary by Huntly; the west by Châtelherault and the Hamiltons; and Edinburgh Castle by Kirkcaldy of Grange and Maitland of Lethington. Despite the Queen's party holding a parliament in the tolbooth in Edinburgh in June 1571, the King's party gradually increased its support as more of the nobles changed their allegiance.

As Moray had not consolidated his powerbase sufficiently, his assassination at Linlithgow on 23 January 1570, organized by the Hamiltons, was not unexpected. Lennox, Darnley's father, was appointed the next regent, but his agenda of revenge against Darnley's murderers did not make him a more popular choice. He was killed at Stirling in 1571, during an attack by the Queen's party. The next official regent was John Erskine, Earl of Mar, who died of natural causes in 1572.

James Douglas, 4th Earl of Morton, dominated the King's party although he was not officially appointed regent until after Mar died. With

Edinburgh Castle

English help, Morton attacked Edinburgh Castle and, on its fall, Kirkcaldy of Grange was hanged. Maitland of Lethington was saved this fate by taking poison after he was captured. In 1571 Archbishop John Hamilton, who was on Mary's side, was captured, and later hanged, during the seizure of Dumbarton Castle by the King's troops. Châtelherault and Huntly agreed to peace terms at Perth in 1573, and over the next three years Argyll (1574), Châtelherault (1575) and Huntly (1576) all died, leaving the governing of the country to Morton, who managed to impose a period of relative tranquillity on the country.

Morton's personality and style of government meant that he created many problems and enemies. Old feuds lingered and, combined with his disastrous financial and pro-English policies, Morton was overthrown in 1578. He was eventually arrested and then executed in 1581 for his part in Darnley's murder.

PAINS AND PLOTS

During Mary's long captivity she suffered from recurrent bouts of illness; she was also either the subject of, or involved with, several conspiracies to free her from her captors. Leonard Dacres, a cousin of the Earl of Northumberland, planned to free her, as did John Hall. Often these plots had a romantic element to them, as various men cast themselves in the role of chivalric hero whose quest was to release Mary from her unjust imprisonment; they all ended disastrously.

Her health also worsened during her imprisonment, a deterioration possibly contributed to by the damp conditions of some of the accommodation and by a lack of regular exercise; she would write in her letters how she had gained weight. There are reports of a rheumatic-like condition, associated with fever, for which she visited the thermal baths at Buxton Wells on several occasions from 1573. Mary stayed at well of

Old Hall, Buxton c.1890?

St Anne's, at what is now the Old Hall Hotel, built by Shrewsbury and Bess in 1573. Her last visit to Buxton was in the summer of 1584. It is claimed that it was Mary who scratched the following couplet on a window pane: 'Buxton, whose warm waters have made thy name famous, perchance I shall visit thee no more – Farewell'.

In the 1580s she had several episodes of dropsy, when her legs became swollen and weak, and throughout the latter years of her life Mary required frequent visits and treatments from a number of physicians. It is also claimed that she suffered from acute intermittent porphyria, into which diagnosis some of her symptoms appear to fall. It is possible she did have this condition, however retrospective diagnoses, based on second hand accounts, are somewhat unreliable.

Although the Duke of Norfolk had been imprisoned in the Tower previously, by 1571 he had not abandoned his hopes of freeing and then marrying Mary. This episode, known as the Ridolfi Plot, was also an international plot, which involved Philip of Spain and the Duke of Alba. When Norfolk was released, Cecil and his spymaster, Sir Francis Walsingham, kept tabs on him and tightened up their screening of Mary's correspondence. Walsingham, like Cecil, was a stern Protestant and determined to use whatever means necessary to rid Elizabeth of Catholic dangers, especially Mary. An Italian banker, Roberto Ridolfi, was a double agent and provided Cecil with the cipher so the plans were revealed easily. Elizabeth was to be captured during a progress; there would be a Catholic revolt, which would free Mary; a Spanish fleet would land, with support from Alba, and Mary would marry Norfolk. Unfortunately for Norfolk, this second incident was more serious and he was executed in June 1572. Mary's response to the proposals had been carefully nuanced, and did not provide sufficient unequivocal evidence to charge her with conspiracy, despite the arrest and questioning of both Leslie, the bishop of Ross, and Norfolk. Cecil and other members of the English parliament urged Elizabeth to execute Mary as well, but she remained reluctant to carry out such an act against an anointed monarch.

The Protestants in England were anxious that Mary remained a focus for Catholics and the following month, August 1572, saw the horrific events of the St Bartholomew's Day Massacre, when 3,000 Protestants in Paris, and a further 12,000 throughout France, were slaughtered. This resulted in a further anti-Catholic backlash in England and Europe, and restrictions against Mary. Her personal staff was reduced to 16 and her movements restricted. At the same time Elizabeth was also dangerously ill with smallpox and many feared she would die.

By 1582, Shrewsbury was in great financial distress: the costs of providing food and board for Mary and her companions had drained his resources. Elizabeth and the state provided only occasional monies. Mary's entourage varied between 15 and 30, and at times had numbered 60. Mary had been a queen and expected certain standards for herself and her people: there were at least five to eight dishes at each meal. There were also rumours that he had become romantically attached to Mary, rumours that were encouraged by his wife Bess. Shrewsbury and Bess had separated due to quarrels about property, money and Mary. In 1584, Sir Ralph Sadler relieved Shrewsbury of his position as Mary's jailor. From January 1585 Mary's last jailor was Sir Amias Paulet, who treated Mary very harshly, limiting her movements and removing her dais and cloth of state, the only two remaining symbols of her royal position.

Francis Throckmorton, a Catholic, was an intermediary between Mary and the Spanish ambassador, Bernardino de Mendoza. He was arrested on Walsingham's orders in November 1583 and, after being tortured on the rack, confessed that the Duke of Guise planned to invade with Spanish and papal support. Throckmorton later retracted his confession but he was executed in 1584. In the same year, William of Orange, who was the leading Protestant in Europe, was assassinated, which led to increased fears about Catholics throughout Europe. A Bond (later the Act for the Queen's Safety) of Association was an oath of loyalty to Elizabeth signed by Protestants, which was drafted by Cecil and Walsingham. It pledged to execute anyone who attempted to injure Elizabeth. Mary made a public declaration supporting the bond, as a demonstration of her loyalty to Elizabeth.

Mary visited Buxton for the last time in July 1584 and in September Sir Ralph Sadler moved her to Wingfield, from where she was transferred to the much loathed Tutbury. The man in charge of these arrangements was Walsingham. There had been another alleged plot, which implicated Thomas

Tutbury Castle

Morgan, a cipher clerk to the French ambassador. Morgan may have also have been another double agent but he was executed on Walsingham's orders. In August, a Jesuit named Creighton was found with papers detailing yet a further Catholic invasion.

Mary had consistently held on to the hope that as her son James matured and took on his personal rule, he would be persuaded to allow her to return to Scotland and even agree to a joint sovereignty. James, despite a brief flirtation with his French cousin, Esmé Stewart, and Catholicism, remained Protestant. Once Elizabeth recognised him as king and offered the tempting prospective of naming him her successor, James informed Mary that, although he would honour her as his mother, he would not offer her joint sovereignty or allow her to return to Scotland. He then signed an Anglo-Scottish peace treaty. This was a great disappointment to Mary; she appears to have been quite desperate during these last two years, responding incautiously to any suggestions and plans to free her from captivity.

ANOTHER DAY, ANOTHER PLOT
The End of the End

In 1585 she was returned to Tutbury, although she had a brief respite at Chartley Hall, which belonged to the Earl of Essex, in December. Paulet replaced Sadler as her jailor, and Walsingham openly checked all her correspondence. He recruited Gilbert Gifford, a refugee, to act as an intermediary between Mary and the French ambassador; he may have been tortured to persuade him to agree. Gifford was backed by Mary's contacts in France, and he brought letters to Mary in January 1586, but Walsingham had designed the code and cipher. Mary's letters, written in code either by Nau, her physician, or Gilbert Curle, her secretary, were placed in a barrel. The barrels were then transported to Gifford, who then passed them to Walsingham.

In June 1586 Mary was in touch with the leader of a group of Catholics, Sir Anthony Babington, who wrote describing details of his plan to assassinate Elizabeth and place Mary on the throne. Babington had been a ward of Shrewsbury and as a young boy had met Mary when she was in Shrewsbury's custody. Mary was aware that if she approved of his plan, and it was a failure, then she would suffer serious consequences: consenting to an assassination plan was clearly against the Bond of Association, and as such was treasonable. She was advised not to reply to Babington and could have informed Paulet about the scheme. However, as James had harshly rejected her hopes for a return to Scotland, her actions were more desperate than ever. She replied to Babington on 17 July giving her support for the plans to invade and release her.

On 11 August 1586, Paulet allowed Mary to go on a stag hunt with members of her staff: Nau, Dominique Bourgoing and her valet Bastien Pages. While they were out, Mary's rooms were searched and the group was confronted and arrested by Sir George Gorges. Mary fell on her knees and prayed, refusing to co-operate, but was eventually moved to Tixall. Babington was arrested and interrogated; he confessed and was executed on 20 September, less than a week after his arrest. On 24 September, Mary was moved to Fortheringhay Castle, which had been used as a prison from the reign of Henry VIII. When Mary left Tixall she called out to beggars: 'I have nothing to give you; I am a beggar as well as you. All is taken from me'.

However, there was still the problem of putting Mary, another monarch, on trial and the international repercussions that would ensue. Cecil

Fotheringhay Castle

and Walsingham did not want Mary to die at this point in case she became a Catholic martyr; they wanted a full trial and a guilty verdict. The Earl of Leicester suggested poisoning Mary. Others, including Elizabeth, felt Mary was frail and unwell and hoped that she would die from natural causes.

The trial started on 15 October and she was accused of treason under the Bond of Association. Evidence of the Babington Plot was produced in the form of copies of Mary's correspondence. Mary, who wore black velvet, as was her custom, was suffering badly from rheumatism and had difficulty walking unaided, but she maintained her dignity throughout the proceedings, and answered the accusations as best she could without the benefit of legal advice or witnesses on her behalf. Some 40 nobles, privy councillors, and judges had been appointed to the court. She admitted to the court that she had become tired of her confinement, and had wished for escape. She acknowledged that she had written to Catholics on the continent and had conspired for the honour of God and Catholics. However, she denied that she had conspired to bring about the death of Elizabeth. During her trial, as Paulet had removed her symbols of royalty, Mary had a crucifix and a picture of Christ beside her, cleverly shifting the focus onto her role as a potential Catholic martyr, which Cecil and Walsingham had wanted to avoid.

On 25 October the verdict was announced: Mary was guilty. Throughout the winter of 1586 and into 1587 Mary awaited Elizabeth's formal signing of her death warrant, which Elizabeth was somewhat reluctant to do in case there were repercussions against her. Paulet wrote to Elizabeth asking for instructions regarding Mary's execution, but Elizabeth delayed. She even wrote to Paulet to ask him to murder Mary discreetly, in order to save her from having to sign the warrant. Rather surprisingly, given his previous attitude towards Mary, he refused to do so; even for him, murder of a queen was a step too far. The warrant was finally signed on 1 February 1587 and, when the news was conveyed to Mary on 4 February, she expressed her relief that she would be finally free of a life which had become so miserable.

Shrewsbury, as Earl Marshal, was in command but he tried to resign this post. Mary was refused access to her chaplain and last sacrament. She spent her last night with her servants, praying and writing, and left instructions for the settling her accounts; her property was to be dispersed to her loyal retainers. These personal gifts and legacies were later removed. Her last letter was to her brother-in-law, Henri III of France. At six o'clock on the day of her execution, 8 February 1587, Mary dressed in a black satin gown over a

Stairs from Fotheringhay, down which Mary ascended on the day of her execution. Now at the Talbot Hotel, Oundle.

velvet petticoat, with a long fine white veil, which reached to her feet and a white cap on her head. She put on a gold rosary and was accompanied by six of her servants into the Great Hall at Fotheringhay where a platform had been erected. She was ordered to remove her outer clothing and so faced the axe wearing a red underskirt. She had chosen this deliberately as the colour red was associated with Catholic martyrs. Afterwards Paulet ordered her clothes and other objects to be burnt to prevent them from later being used for veneration and as relics.

The death warrant was read out and Mary prayed aloud in Latin and English; the executioner Bull asked her forgiveness as was customary. Covering her eyes with a gold-fringed cloth she laid her head upon the block. Mary's last words were: 'Into thy hands, O Lord, I commend my spirit'. Three blows of the axe later the executioner held up her head by her hair, only to find that Mary wore a wig and her head fell from his grasp onto the floor.

Her severed head, from which a wax death mask was taken, was displayed on a black cushion, and her body quickly embalmed. She was not buried until 30 July when her remains were moved to Peterborough and interred opposite Catherine of Aragon. The burial took place in private at night; the next day there was a low-key public service and procession.

There was very little reaction in Scotland although James made a public show of sorrow, at the same time being careful not to offend or criticise Elizabeth. There was a charade of outrage from Elizabeth who claimed it was all a dreadful mistake and she had punished those involved. A Requiem Mass was conducted at Notre Dame in Paris on 12 March, accompanied by some displays of grief from the Valois court.

However, within a short time of her death, the publication of tributes and pamphlets started, some in England and others in France, in which Mary was cast either as a Jezebel or as a romantic martyr. Opinions about the dramatic events of Mary's life and death continue to divide along comparable lines, and have doubtless fuelled claims about her many ghosts.

AFTERMATH

Once James VI, son of Mary and Darnley, succeeded Elizabeth of England in 1603, he united the crowns of the two kingdoms. By doing so, peacefully and by mutual consent, Mary's heir(s) achieved more than any previous kings either of Scots or of England who had attempted invasions of each other's countries: '… now she triumphs by death, that her stock might thereafter burgeon with fresh fruits…' However, although united by a common monarch, the two kingdoms remained constitutionally independent and retained separate parliaments until 1707.

In 1612 James VI had his mother's body brought from Peterborough Cathedral and reinterred in the south aisle of the Lady Chapel in Westminster Abbey, London. He commissioned Cornelius and William Cure to design and produce an elaborate effigy of her wearing state robes. This act may have been to absolve him of any guilt by association in his mother's death and the fact that he did very little to prevent it; however it also emphasised strongly his own legitimacy as king of both Scotland and England and enhanced his regal image. He later ordered the demolition of Fotheringhay Castle, the place where Mary had been executed. James VI encouraged a positive reassessment of Mary's life and helped promote her veneration as his 'birth' or 'natural' mother. The commissioning of sculptured effigies to celebrate monarchy was new in Britain in the 16th century, but had been used earlier in France and Florence. The effigy is made from white marble and cost around £2000. The figure of Mary is positioned under an elaborate canopy, wearing a close-fitting coif, a laced ruff, and a long mantle fastened by a brooch, her hands together as if in prayer. The Scottish lion crowned is positioned at her feet. The tomb of Margaret, Countess of Lennox, on which is a kneeling figure of her son, Lord Darnley, is next to Mary. The meaning behind the inscription is clear: Mary was innocent, pious, courageous, honourable, and beautiful. A translation of the inscription on Mary's tomb in the abbey reads:

'To God, the best and greatest. To her good memory, and in eternal hope. MARY STUART, QUEEN OF SCOTS, Dowager Queen of France, daughter of James V of Scotland, sole heir and great granddaughter of Henry VII, King of England, through his elder daughter Margaret, (who was joined in marriage to James IV of Scotland): great-great-granddaughter of Edward IV, King of England through his eldest daughter of Elizabeth [of York]: wife of Francis II, King of France: sure and certain heiress to the crown of England while she lived: mother of James, most puissant sovereign

Mary's effigy, viewed from above, Westminster Abbey

of Great Britain. She was sprung from royal and most ancient stock, linked on both paternal and maternal side with the greatest princes of Europe, abundantly endowed with most excellent gifts and adornments both of soul and body; yet, such are the manifold changes of human fortune, that, after she had been detained in custody for more or less twenty years, and had courageously and vigorously, (but vainly), fought against the obloquies of her foes, the mistrust of the faint-hearted, and the crafty devices of her mortal enemies, she was at last struck down by the axe (an unheard-of precedent, outrageous to royalty) and, despising the world, conquering death (the executioner being wearied), commending to Christ her Saviour the salvation of her soul; to James her son the hope of a kingdom and posterity, and to all who witnessed her unhappy murder an ensample of endurance, she piously, patiently and courageously submitted her royal neck to the accursed axe, and exchanged the fate of a transitory life for the eternity of an heavenly kingdom, on 8 February, year of Christ 1587, in the 46th year of her age.

If splendour of birth, if rare beauty of form, a mind innocent of vice, an unbesmirched honour, the power of an invincible spirit, a brilliance of intelligence, a hope (springing from piety) of divine consolation, if probity of character, endurance of harsh restraint, if majesty, pure goodness, and a bounteous hand: if all these were able to avoid the pallor-inducing, fulminating thunderbolts of fortune (which seek out mountains and holy places) she would not have died untimely, according to her fated destiny, nor would her effigy be made sorrowful with mourning genii [winged cherubs].

Mistress of Scotland by law, of France by marriage, of England expectation, thus blest, by a three-fold right, with a three-fold crown; happy, ah, only too happy, had she routed the tumult of war, and, even at a late hour, won over the neighbouring forces. But she perished that she might possess the land: now she triumphs by death, that her stock might thereafter burgeon with fresh fruits. Conquered, she was unconquerable, nor could the dungeon detain her; slain, yet deathless, imprisoned, yet not a prisoner. Thus does the pruned vine groan with a greater abundance of grapes, and the cut jewel gleams with a brilliant splendour.

So seeds, lying hidden through many days, gradually spring up from the fruitful earth. With blood did Jehovah ratify his covenant with his people, with blood did our fathers propitiate the divine powers; with blood were sprinkled those household gods who anger was assuaged; with blood has the land been stained which lately had yielded. Forbear, O God, it is enough: put an end to these unutterable woes. May the day of [their own] death swoop upon the death-dealers. May it be forbidden to slaughter monarchs, that henceforward the land of Britain may never more flow with purple blood. May this precedent of the violent murder of the anointed Queen come to naught; may the instigator and perpetrator rush headlong to destruction.

Should she, after her own death, be vindicated by all the well-disposed, then executioners, tortures, gaols and gallows, all would cease. The Queen accomplished that journey which the heavenly powers allotted. God bestowed happy times, hard times. She gave birth, fate being propitious, to the excellent James, whom Pallas [Athena], the Muses, Diana, and the Fates revere. Great in marriage, greater still in lineage, greatest of all in her progeny, here lies buried the daughter, bride and mother of kings. God grant that her sons, and all who are descended from her, may hereafter behold the cloudless days of eternity. Mourning, I wrote this H.N.[Henry, Earl of Northampton].

Christ suffered also for us, leaving us an example, that ye should follow His steps.1.Pet[er].2.21.

Who, when He was reviled, reviled not again; when He suffered, He threatened not; but committed Himself to Him that judgeth righteously.1.Pet.2.22 [actually verse 23]'

James also commissioned an effigy and monument of Elizabeth to be placed in the north aisle of the Lady Chapel at Westminster. James had to demonstrate his loyalty to Elizabeth, again to validate his legitimacy as her heir, as well as to Mary: Mary was his biological mother but she had no power, Elizabeth was therefore cast as his political mother. The effigy, particularly amongst those who were critical of James's policies, may have enhanced and emphasised Elizabeth's reputation as Gloriana, but it is half the size of Mary's and cost about half the price. Elizabeth's effigy resembles portraits of her in old age. The recumbent figure, under a canopy, is supported by four lions, and wears a ruff and royal robe. Her feet rest on a lion, she holds a sceptre in her right hand and an orb in her left, and the inscription to her memory is short and to the point. It reads:

'Sacred to memory: Religion to its primitive purity restored, peace settled, money restored to its just value, domestic rebellion quelled, France relieved when involved with intestine divisions; the Netherlands supported; the Spanish Armada vanquished; Ireland almost lost by rebels, eased by routing the Spaniard; the revenues of both universities much enlarged by a Law of Provisions; and lastly, all England enriched. Elizabeth, a most prudent governor 45 years, a victorious and triumphant Queen, most strictly religious, most happy, by a calm and resigned death at her 70th year left her mortal remains, till by Christ's Word they shall rise to immortality, to be deposited in the Church [the Abbey], by her established and lastly founded. She died the 24th of March, Anno 1602 [this is Old Style dating, now called 1603], of her reign the 45th year, of her age the 70th.

To the eternal memory of Elizabeth queen of England, France and Ireland, daughter of King Henry VIII, grand-daughter of King Henry VII, great-grand-daughter to King Edward IV. Mother of her country, a nursing-mother to religion and all liberal sciences, skilled in many languages, adorned with excellent endowments both of body and mind, and excellent for princely virtues beyond her sex. James, king of Great Britain, France and Ireland,

Mary Queen of Scots © Blairs Museum
(Reproduced by kind permission of Blairs Museum)

Stirling
Castle (below)

Linlithgow
Palace
(above)

Hermitage
Castle
(left)

Mary Queen of
Scots House, Jedburgh
(right and below)
© Scottish Borders Council
Museum Service (below)

Palace of
Holyroodhouse
(left)

Craigmillar
Castle
(above)

Borthwick
Castle (above)

Lochleven
Castle (left)

Craignethan Castle (above)

Bolton Castle (above) © Bolton Castle (Reproduced by kind permission of Bolton Castle)

Queen Elizabeth I 1575 © National Portrait Gallery, London
(Reproduced by kind permission of National Portrait Gallery, London)

Portrait believed to be of Mary Queen of Scots, Alonso Sanchez Coello © Devonshire Collection

Wingfield
Manor
(top)

Turret House and
Manor Lodge,
Sheffield
(right and bottom)

Dragsholm Slot
(Castle)
(right)
© Dragsholm Slot
(Reproduced by kind
permission of
Dragsholm Slot)

James Hepburn,
4th Earl of
Bothwell
(study of
mummified head)
by Otto Bache 1861
(Below)
© National Galleries
of Scotland
(Reproduced by kind
permission of National
Galleries of Scotland)

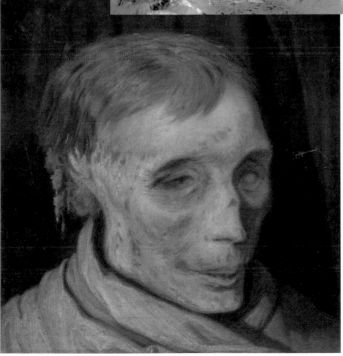

Tutbury Castle (above) © Tutbury Castle
(Reproduced by kind permission of Tutbury Castle)

IN MEMORY OF
MARY STUART, QUEEN OF SCOTS,
BEHEADED IN THE GREAT HALL
OF FOTHERINGHAY CASTLE
8TH FEBRUARY 1586/7

THIS MEMORIAL WAS PLACED HERE
BY THE STUART HISTORY SOCIETY
IN 1964

Plaque, site of Fotheringhay Castle (above)

Fotheringhay
Castle (above)

Talbot Hotel,
Oundle and stair
from Fotheringhay
Castle in the hotel
(top and left)

Execution of Mary Queen of Scots c.1613 (above) © National Galleries of Scotland
(Reproduced by kind permission of National Galleries of Scotland)

Peterborough Cathedral

Mary Queen of Scots (above) © Blairs Museum

(Reproduced by kind permission of Blairs Museum)

Mary Queen of Scots' death mask (above), Mary Queen of Scots Visitor Centre, Jedburgh.
© Scottish Borders Council Museum Service

Mary Queen of Scots' tomb, Westminster Abbey © Dean and Chapter of Westminster
(Reproduced by kind permission of Dean and Chapter of Westminster)

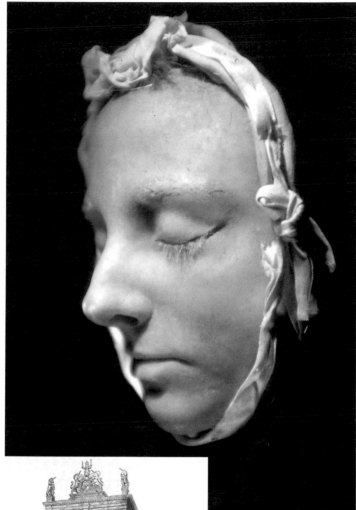

Mary Queen of Scots' death
mask (above)
© Lennoxlove House Ltd.
Licensor www.scran.ac.uk

Mary Queen of Scots' tomb,
Westminster Abbey, 1845 (left)

Study for The Execution of Mary Queen of Scots, Ford Madox Brown (WA1977.21)
© Ashmolean Museum, University of Oxford

hath devoutly and justly erected this monument to her whose virtues and kingdoms he inherits.'

On the base of the monument it reads: 'Partners in throne and grave, here we sleep, Elizabeth and Mary, sisters, in hope of the Resurrection.'

The two great rivals, who never met in life, are at least symbolically positioned near each other after death.

MARY'S LEGACY AND REPUTATION

Mary, Mary quite contrary
How does your garden grow?
With silver bells and cockle shells
And pretty maids all in a row.

When Mary died in 1587 it was the start of the rehabilitation of her reputation, as much by her own performance as by the actions and words of her enemies such as Elizabeth, Cecil and Buchanan and her eulogisers such as Leslie, Blackwood and Haywood. Mary's choice to wear scarlet, which she must have known would be exposed, under her sombre black gown was deliberate. Her Protestant opponents, primarily Cecil, ordered that everything she wore or was used at the execution was to be burnt to prevent their later use as relics. He need not have bothered, as Mary's legacy as a tragic victim, romantic heroine, religious martyr, and latterly as a ghost or spectre, had started even before her death, with the publication of diametrically opposed accounts of her life.

George Buchanan's defence of Mary's abdication, and the role of the Confederate Lords, *Detection of the Douings of Marie,* was published in 1567. As Buchanan was also heavily involved in the creation and counterfeiting of the Casket Letters, it is hardly surprising that his Mary was presented as a 'poisoning witch', who killed her husband Darnley. John Leslie, Bishop of Ross, and a loyal supporter, had a very different account of Mary's life up to 1567. In *Defence of the Honour of [...] Marie*, published in 1568, he presented her as a 'careful, tender mother' who led a 'godly and virtuous life'. These contrasting contemporary interpretations would anticipate the continued, contradictory, opinions about Mary.

Mary has transcended historical fact. From being a queen whose actions ranged from the sensible and pragmatic to the sentimental and perilous, she has become a character of romanticised myth, fitting the purpose or needs of the writers and centuries. Along with changing the spelling of her family name from 'Stewart' to 'Stuart', Mary was a Catholic martyr in the 16th century; the founding mother of the Stewart Jacobite line in the 18th century; a beautiful but helpless woman in the 19th century; to more recently, either an unfortunate queen, unable to manage male–dominated politics and society, or as a ghost or spectre, merely a vague, indistinct image. Novels, poems, plays, paintings, operas and films have all exposed and portrayed Mary's life for public scrutiny, consumption, entertainment or education. The construction and durability of her narrative has transformed her from harlot to heroine, from an anointed but inadequate monarch to a victim of circumstances, unfairly executed. Her reputation has undergone many revisions and, although for many Mary's role as Catholic martyr may no longer be so relevant, her story still survives not only through words and images, but also through oral testimony and claims made about many sightings of her ghostly spirit. Her life may have been dramatic, but her death, and the manner in which she died, has ensured that Mary has continued to be remembered and visible, even if, in some cases, only as a shadow.

As soon as Mary died, her life and reputation became the focus for critics of Elizabeth and her Protestant regime in England – even the French who had remained remarkably noncommittal during her captivity, permitted some expression of dismay. On the day after the funeral service held at Notre Dame in Paris, a Latin poem depicting Elizabeth as a murderer and Mary as a martyr, was attached to the door of the cathedral. A translation of the poem title was 'A Poem Concerning the Parricides of the Jezebel of England, Addressed to the Pious Ghost of Mary Queen of Scots' – perhaps the first mention of Mary as a ghost? The writer was Adam Blackwood, a Catholic Scot based in Paris, and he also wrote *Martyre de la Royne d'Escosse* and probably also *La Mort de la Royne d'Escosse*, which were printed in Paris around 1587/9, and used eye witness accounts of Mary's death from her servants, primarily one of her physicians and two of her ladies: Elizabeth Curle and Jane Kennedy. Blackwood's account is critical of Protestants, John Knox and others, and particularly Elizabeth, whom he portrayed, in sharp contrast to the beautiful and pious Mary, as a vile and wicked murderer, born of an illegitimate and incestuous relationship. Other publications and martyrologies, including Robert Verstegan's *book of saintly martyrs* (1587), took up the theme of Mary's transformation into a Catholic martyr. Books, ballads and plays, in French and Latin, were in circulation in France, Spain, Italy and Belgium from the late 1580s; but their purpose to encourage European Catholic monarchs to avenge Mary's death largely failed. English propaganda about the events of 1587, such as the account of her execution by English Protestant Robert Wyngfield, was successful in persuading the French king Henri III and Pope Sixtus V to do little more than issue verbal protestations, despite general concerns about Protestant heresy.

James VI (and I) encouraged William Camden to complete his *Annals*, a history of Elizabeth's reign. Camden's account of the period, interestingly entitled *History of the Life and Death of Mary Stuart, Queen of Scotland*, rather than *A History of Elizabeth Queen of England*, published in 1624, contradicted Buchanan's version of events. According to Camden, who researched the documents and archives meticulously, Mary was loyal to her religion and was a victim of her nobles in general and in particular, her half brother, James, Earl of Moray. Camden's interpretation complemented James's position that as his birth mother, Mary was beautiful, virtuous, pious, legitimate and committed to her faith, which only served to validate his accession to the English throne

In the 18th century, her popularity as a dramatic character increased, coinciding with the development and popularity of historical romance and fiction. English writers no longer defended Elizabeth and Protestantism, even if their material proved controversial initially. Elizabeth was no longer Good Queen Bess, or Gloriana of Spenser's *Faerie Queen*. English playwright, John Banks, wrote *The Island Queens* or *The Death of Mary Queen of Scots*, in 1684 following his controversial play about Lady Jane Grey, who was regarded as a Protestant martyr. However, both plays were unpopular on political grounds during the reign of William and Mary. *The Island Queens* was banned but by the early 1700s it found an appreciative audience, particularly once the Stewarts were no longer on the throne. Indeed Mary's story was given more drama by being linked to the ultimately futile Jacobite cause. Mary's life, as the mother of the Stewart Jacobites, was presented as romantic fiction, even if the writers claimed their works were based on historical fact. Eliza Haywood's *Mary Stuart, Queen of Scots, Being a Secret History of her Life and the Real Causes of All Her Misfortunes* published in 1725, claimed to be a history, not romance. It was a translation of a 17th-century French work and other material and, although categorised as non-fiction, it was as dramatic as the polemical publications by Leslie and Blackwood.

An Italian, Vittorio Alfieri, published his play *Maria Stuarda* in 1778. He and Louise of Stolberg-Gedern, who was the wife of Charles Edward Stewart, the claimant of the Stewart Jacobite line, would later become lovers but he wrote the play when he met Louise and Charles in Florence. Sophia Lee's *The Recess: or a Tale of Other Times* published in 1783-1785, is a novel set in Elizabethan times, and gives a sentimental account of Mary's loss of political power and position. The main narrators are fictional twin daughters of Mary, who herself is portrayed as being saintly, even, ironically, virginal.

In the 19th century, Mary and her story continued to beguile writers and prove a rewarding framework for their own interpretation and imagination, sometimes with little regard for factional accuracy. Friedrich Schiller's 1800 play *Maria Stuart*, portrays a fictional event: a meeting between Mary and Elizabeth. In keeping with the perpetual theme of opposites, Elizabeth's character represents more 'male' characteristics: devious, determined, virginal and sanctimonious, and certainly not maternal; Mary's as more feminine: straightforward, trusting, sexual but pious, and maternal.

His Elizabeth is unscrupulous and his Mary a victim of circumstance. Modern versions of the play (and opera) have concentrated on the general themes of unjust imprisonment, tyranny and religious extremism, which have resonated at various times with 20th and 21st-century audiences, rather than concentrating solely on the religious tensions of the 16th century. Walter Scott's 1820 novel *The Abbot* covers the period when Mary was held at Lochleven. Although sympathetic to Mary, Scott was critical of Catholicism. In order to address this contradictory problem Scott focused on Mary's role in producing a legitimate, and Protestant, prince-king, who would unite the crowns in 1603, as her greatest achievement, thereby neutralising her 'heretical' religious beliefs.

Schiller's 1800 play *Maria Stuart* was adapted into an opera by Gaetano Donizetti and as with novels and plays, Mary has been the inspiration for other composers from the 19th century and later: Robert Schumann, Thea Musgrave, Louis Niedermeyer, Mike Oldfield, and Sandy Denny of Fairport Convention, up to Dougie MacLean's 2010 song *Mary Queen of Scots* inspired by a spooky visit to Fotheringhay.

In the 20th century biographies, novels, films and plays about Mary have continued to prove a popular subject, particularly with female novelists: Jean Plaidy (*Royal Road to Fotheringhay, The Captive Queen of Scots* and *Mary Queen of Scots: The Fair Devil of Scotland*) in the 1960s and 1970s; Philippa Gregory (*The Other Queen*) in 2009 and Margaret George (*Mary Queen of Scots and the Isles*) in 2012, to name but a few. Throughout these novels, Mary is consistently presented as a woman of contradictions: naïve but manipulative in her relations with men; ambitious but consistently loyal to her faith; beautiful but dangerous; poignant but pathetic.

In 1936, John Ford directed an RKO film adaptation of Maxwell Anderson's play *Mary of Scotland* with Katherine Hepburn as Mary. As usual Mary was depicted as a martyr but, more unusually and perhaps inaccurately, Bothwell was portrayed as a romantic hero. The film was, despite its subject matter, not a critical or box office success. Katherine Hepburn, who was Mary, was labelled 'box office poison' after its release. *Das Herz der Konigin* (*The Heart of the Queen*) is a German film from 1940, which used selective events from Mary's story as wartime anti-British propaganda. In 1971 *Mary Queen of Scots*, with Vanessa Redgrave as Mary and Glenda Jackson as Elizabeth, was released. It is loosely based on the Schiller play and Donizetti opera, but with more soap than drama. The tensions between the two rivals are given voice during imaginary meetings. In the film, Mary's imprisonment, in luxurious comfort, reduces her to a needy and demanding woman with no purpose, only regaining her regal dignity at the end, sanitising and simplifying the reality of her years in captivity.

The play *Mary Queen of Scots Got Her Head Chopped Off* by Liz Lochhead, first produced in 1987, explores a variety of myths and stereotypes, male and female identities and characteristics, and power and politics, again using the contrast between the lives and experiences of the two queens. As in other depictions, Elizabeth uses masculine behaviour in order to control those around her; Mary uses her sexuality and vulnerability to achieve the same. However, the schism between Catholicism and Protestantism is also an important main focus, rather than just the tension between the queens, and is illustrated by the legacy of continued sectarianism.

Many versions of Mary's story, her image and legacy, have entered the minds and memories of the wider public via different forms of media. Since the 16th century, her life has been repeated, adapted, altered and dramatized in words. Her visual image has also been subject to similar modifications and inventions. Immediately after her death, as was common, a wax cast of Mary's head was made. It has been claimed that there were four masks, which would have been white and undecorated. Only two survive, although they appear non-identical, and both have had eyelashes, eyebrows and some paint added. The version at Mary Queen of Scots House in Jedburgh, allegedly found in Peterborough Abbey, has been more than a little enhanced. It has red hair and lips and what appears to be a nice pale-blue eye shadow – hardly in keeping with 16th century cosmetics. It displays Mary as a beautiful, young woman, who is at peace; rather than the middle-aged woman she really was in 1587. Mary was 44 when she died; she had been held in reduced circumstances and freedom for 19 years; she had suffered many episodes of ill-health and complained about her weight gain due to lack of exercise. It seems unlikely that she was a beautiful young corpse.

By the early 19th century, Madame Tussaud had produced a wax model of Mary and her execution that was popular with the public. A model of Bonnie Prince Charlie was also a favourite; quite possibly as a reaction to the incumbent Hanoverian monarchy. Although well liked, George III's illness had rendered him a puppet king; his son, the Prince Regent, was universally detested. Once again romance proved more acceptable – or entertaining – than reality for the general public. A figure of Mary is still on display at Madame Tussaud's in London, wearing the black dress, the white ruff and frilled cap (reminiscent of the *deuil blanc*), and prominently-placed crucifix, based on the 1578 miniature portrait of Mary by Nicholas Hilliard.

Mary had portraits done of her from life, but most images of her were done as copies of originals or from the artist's imagination. As with all portraiture, Mary's included deliberate motifs and symbols which emphasised her beauty, her grief, her power and authority, her immorality, her privations, her dignity and her Catholicism. Amongst the most famous are those done by, or attributed to, the French artist François Clouet. His chalk drawing of her from life, as the future Dauphine of France in c.1555, and his oil portrait based on the sketch, c.1558, show Mary as a young queen. In the colour version she is wearing a French-style red dress, embroidered with pearls, beautiful and dignified. However, a more iconic image associated with Mary, probably also by Clouet, is as a young widow wearing the *deuil blanc*. Mary's face is very white, even transparent, and her expression sombre: perhaps anticipating the ghost she would become? In mourning at this point, Mary's life had undergone a huge transformation and her future was uncertain, although she could never have anticipated how badly events would unfold.

There are few portraits of Mary done during her adult years in Scotland, and certainly none wearing a crown to depict her royal position. A miniature, produced around 1565, has a slightly older Mary, in a black dress with pearls and a striking feathered hat, which may have been done by Clouet. There is another colour portrait c.1565 by an unknown artist, which is claimed to have been done in Scotland, perhaps to mark her marriage to Darnley, as she appears to hold what might be her *deuil blanc* or handkerchief in her right hand. These portraits depict Mary in her last years as a queen, but still with authority and sovereignty. During the crisis of 1567, less flattering images of Mary were produced: the notorious and insulting placard, which depicted her as a mermaid and prostitute, bore little resemblance to her previous regal, image.

Another iconic image of Mary, much copied, is the Hilliard miniature dated 1578. It was painted from life, as Mary sat for Hilliard in 1576 while she was in the custody of the Earl of Shrewsbury. In it Mary wears a black gown with a high white ruff and her ever-present white cap, and a small gold crucifix. There are reports that Mary herself distributed copies of the Sheffield portrait to her supporters and staff.

Some full-length copies have Mary holding a rosary as well as wearing a crucifix, although others omit the Catholic emblems: instead of a rosary Mary holds a white handkerchief. In a full size copy, which is now at Blairs Museum near Aberdeen (see colour section), Mary is presented as a tall, majestic figure, with a fur-edged pelisse in front of her black gown, wearing the standard small crucifix suspended from a black ribbon. In her right hand she holds a larger crucifix with an image of the crucified Christ carved in ivory; in her left she is holding a small prayer book. Behind Mary there is a representation of her execution and the royal coat of arms of Scotland are in the upper left corner. The portrait/copy was most likely done after the accession of James VI to the English throne in 1603, although it has the date 1587. After her death, Mary's portraits increasingly show her regaining her regal status: tall and majestic, a beautiful and peaceful figure, not ravaged by years of captivity. As befitted the interest in Mary during the reign of another queen – Victoria – several versions of the Hilliard portrait were exhibited together in London in 1889 in order to contrast the varying adaptations and embellishments.

As Mary's story was rewritten as dramatized fiction during the 18th and 19th century, so too was her image. The engravings and paintings produced in the late decades of the 18th century and throughout the 1800s, were not portraits but *tableau vivant*, posed imaginings of particular events from Mary's life. Gavin Hamilton's painting of Mary resigning her throne was exhibited in 1776 and was commissioned by James Boswell. Hamilton said of his portrayal: 'beauty in distress is what I mean to convey' and Mary's story and image contained both.

An engraving dated 1779 shows her with James VI, and is based on a painting by Frederico Zuccaro. Jacques Rigaud published c. 1790 a series six etchings depicting the end of Mary's life, including her execution. Robert Cromek's 1798 engraving shows her being abducted by Bothwell in 1567 and was made for an edition of William Robertson's *History of Scotland*. An engraving by Robert Dunkerton, published in 1816, shows Mary with Darnley. John Burnet's engraving, from a painting by Sir William Allan, depicts Mary being admonished by John Knox. Mary is shown holding her head in her hands, either exhausted or ashamed. Allan had exhibited his original work in 1823 and took his inspiration from Sir Walter Scott's version of Mary's history, which while being sympathetic to Mary was less sympathetic to her faith.

Another famous painting by Sir William Allan is the *Murder of Rizzio*, exhibited in 1833. Here Mary appears less downcast, less a victim, than during her meeting with Knox. Left of centre, she struggles and is physically restrained; but is still powerless to prevent the murder. Another version of the same event, by Rothwell, is far less violent in its depiction of the murder. His engraving, *Death of Rizzio*, also from the early 19th century, has Mary in the centre, in white, waving her hands somewhat ineffectually as the conspirators appear to ask her permission to carry out the murder. A depiction by Andrew Duncan, published in 1830, of Mary with Pierre de Chastelard playing the lute, is also based on an earlier work. In it Mary is wearing the black gown, white ruff and crucifix associated with her portrait by Hilliard.

Ford Madox Brown painted his smaller *Study for 'The Execution of Mary, Queen of Scots'* (see colour section) and the larger, full painting *Execution of*

Mary Queen of Scots in 1840-2; the final painting was one of his first major exhibited works. In the smaller study Madox Brown portrays a head resting on a pillow and does not give us a full view of Mary, but in the full study he depicts Mary in black holding a crucifix in her left hand, whilst listening attentively to an Anglican priest reading scripture – echoing many of the usual motifs. Slightly more unusually, however, is that rather than wearing her traditional white cap, Mary's head is not covered and her hair is loose. Her gown, although the standard black, is positioned off the shoulder, without a ruff, exposing her décolletage. Madox Brown's Mary is both more mature and more sexual than other portrayals. With bare flesh and accentuated hips, she holds a finger rather coquettishly to her lips, and appears more ambiguous, less the innocent victim, than in many other portrayals. Although completed well before the formation of the Pre-Raphaelite Movement, of which Madox

Mary (engraving, 1885)

Brown was never a full member, the painting does share some of its radical aims and desires to reject what were the conventions of the time.

Farewell to France and *Execution of Mary Queen of Scots* are two famous works by Robert Herdman, more in keeping with the conventional romanticised view of Mary. In 1867, Herdman was commissioned by the Glasgow Art Union to do four paintings illustrating events from Mary's life. In *Farewell to France* Mary is depicted looking sadly towards France, not excited about her future in Scotland, her ladies kneeling beside her trying to comfort her. In the *Execution of Mary, Queen of Scots*, Mary is depicted, again young and beautiful, going toward her death in her customary black gown, with a flash of her red petticoat showing underneath. Her ladies are kneeling behind her and her executioners standing in front. Herdman's Mary is dignified and serene, heroic and saintly. By the late 1800s, Mary had reached the height of her popularity as a romantic figure both in words and pictures: she was majestic, beautiful and dignified. Her human failings were glossed over and depictions and descriptions of her life, and particularly of her death, had allowed Mary to regain her reputation, position and beauty.

Another stage in Mary's legacy was her transformation into a hard-working ghost that gave her story another means of transmission and persistence. Reports of her spectre could be given legitimacy or authenticity as they related to specific places and locations associated with events in Mary's life. Ghosts are recognised as symbols that memorialize tragic events – particularly deaths – and often have an attachment to precise physical locations. Mary's ghosts – or non-specific apparitions – do not usually seem to have appeared on particular dates or anniversaries, unlike some other notable ghosts. She does not appear to be evil or dangerous, more wistful and sad. But stories about her ghost are numerous and still of interest to people. However or whatever way Mary has appeared – as a painting, waxwork, death mask, dramatic performance, or ghost – it has allowed her life, her story, to continue to be remembered and discussed. Whatever way you prefer your Mary, you certainly can't escape her…

MARY'S GHOSTS

Stories about Mary's apparition – mostly complete with head, although occasionally without – are both popular and numerous. Alleged sightings have been claimed for a number of the castles, halls, or other form of accommodation, that she visited in Scotland and for almost all of those in England where she was held captive. As might be expected, many of the sightings are associated with places where Mary experienced a dramatic, and often unhappy, event or period of her life, such as the Palace of Holyroodhouse, Edinburgh Castle or Lochleven Castle in Scotland, and Tutbury in England. However, perhaps less understandably, there are also claims made about a female apparition identified as Mary in places that she did not visit or was imprisoned, for example Eilean Donan Castle and the Tower of London. Finally, Mary also stayed at several locations that do appear to have been visited by her ghostly spirit, including Niddry and Terregles Castle and Dundrennan Abbey. Some, of course, have their own ghost stories, which do not feature Mary.

Although some of the manifestations of Mary's ghost are quite vague – a presence, a sound or a light rather than a recognisable figure – other apparitions have more specific detail, although perhaps not always enough for a certain identification as Mary. The apparitions appear as an adult female, often beautiful, sometimes wearing blue, white or even pink. In a number of the descriptions from English locations, the figure has been recorded as wearing a black gown with a white collar – very similar to, and perhaps influenced by, the famous Hilliard miniature. A few stories, such as those about Craignethan and Dalkeith, also claim that the figure is headless.

Many ghost stories do not have a named character or event at their core, but those that do might have more authenticity or be more believable. These usually relate to a dramatic and/or violent event, most usually the untimely or violent death of an individual. The events of Mary's life and death, including her visits to different places, are well documented; therefore many locations have a legitimate connection to her story and have a reason why her spirit might wish to remain. Undoubtedly the drama, the romance, and the tragedy of Mary's life give some explanation as to why her spirit might be troubled and not at rest and yet be connected to places she visited. Although she was executed at Fotheringhay her ghost seems to have translated, along with the stairs, windows and other materials from Fotheringhay to the Talbot Hotel in nearby Oundle, which was built from its remains. Interestingly, the site of Fotheringhay Castle, itself, does not appear to be haunted by Mary.

Mary haunting the place where she was executed (or at least where the materials from the castle now are) may not be surprising: what event could more traumatic and violent events are usually the genesis of a ghost. But why all the others? And when did the stories about her ghost appear: soon after her death or much later? In the case of the Manor Lodge at Sheffield, the stories were not recorded until the 1930s (although may have been circulating long before this) but many accounts are not so specific about when the claims started. Accounts of Mary's ghosts may have been repeated and evolved over the intervening centuries or they may only have appeared or been repeated in more recent decades – or even years, because of the widespread use of the internet.

Belief in ghosts is not, of course, a modern phenomena; in the 16th and 17th centuries, some people accused of witchcraft confessed to seeing and communicating with ghosts of family members or long-deceased individuals, often in the company of fairies. With the impact and influence of the Protestant church in the 16th and 17th centuries, and 18th-century rationalism and the rise of science, belief in supernatural spirits declined. But paradoxically, interest in proving – or disproving – the existence of spirits using science increased, particularly after the heavy loss of life during World War I. Spiritualism, mediums, and parapsychology have all been used to demonstrate the reality of ghosts from the late 19th century, but the vast majority of us continue not to experience ghostly manifestations. It has been suggested that those who claim to have witnessed ghostly activity are more susceptible to suggestion; if they are told about alleged manifestations they are more likely to report similar occurrences themselves – or at least interpret particular experiences or phenomena as being signs of ghostly activity.

So are the stories about Mary's ghost believable and is there a rational explanation about how a deceased person can haunt so many different places? While not wishing to sound too cynical, some of the 'stories' have been used to help promote individual sites, particularly in a commercial way. They add mystery and drama to the history of the buildings and so may add extra interest or a frisson of anticipation for some visitors, especially those who actively believe in the reality of ghosts and spirits. Alternatively, however, many places are uncomfortable even with the idea of a ghost, so there may be stories still to be unearthed.

That is not to suggest that some of the stories are entirely fictional or have been deliberately created, but, as with other ghost stories, there is a tendency for people to try to provide explanations or agency for experiences and/or events which they cannot explain. Event A: documented evidence that Mary stayed at X location; event B: a person experienced an unexpected noise or sensation at X location, perhaps on numerous occasions. For those who link the two events, a conclusion would be that they had witnessed a manifestation of Mary's spirit. (Of course many others would have dismissed the sounds or sensations as coincidental or insignificant.) In such a manner, stories about Mary's ghosts were probably started and subsequently transmitted – initially orally but later in print and now circulating freely on the World Wide Web. Like all good legends and myths, they have evolved over time, and later claims of sightings are used to provide necessary confirmation.

Nevertheless, the stories about Mary's ghosts are in keeping with the overall tradition of preserving and reinventing her story and legacy, whether by Catholic propaganda; portraiture – from life or through imagined scenes; or plays and operas. Much of what has been written or portrayed about Mary has been fictionalised or dramatized, and so, within that context, these stories about her ghost are no less legitimate or less plausible than other interpretations or depictions. It is worth noting that stories about Mary's ghost are much more numerous and wide-ranging than those about Anne Boleyn, Lady Jane Grey or Catherine Howard – all of whom were also brutally executed. Mary also apparently haunts far more sites than her great adversary Elizabeth. Even after death, Mary appears to have trounced and surpassed her rival. If you believe in ghosts then the stories will be credible; if you don't then they are simply interesting stories about Mary and her enduring legacy.

Whatever the truth, there are numerous 'credible' accounts covering 25 or so sites, more if Mary's contemporaries are also included. 'Credible' in this context means within the parameters of usual ghostly phenomena and traditions, more specifically that Mary both visited the site, that some violent or traumatic event happened while she was there, and thereafter unexplained manifestations occurred, not least the sighting of an apparition matching Mary's description, or at least other unexplained activity, such as footsteps or voices from unoccupied areas, doors opening and closing by themselves, electrical appliances being interfered with, sudden drops in temperature, people thinking an unseen person is pushing past them, or (minimally) people have uncomfortable feelings about a room or place.

As will be seen, many places Mary visited have ghostly or supernatural tales not connected to her.

In the following accounts it should be assumed that all supernatural manifestations are reputed or alleged, and no claim is made as to their veracity. The over use of these terms can make the accounts clumsy so omission should not be taken as a indication of an account either being factual or credible.

Visitor information about the sites listed in the next chapters can be found in the Places of Interest, along with information on other sites associated with Mary.

MARY'S GHOSTS IN SCOTLAND

Linlithgow Palace, where Mary was born in 1542, is a splendid royal palace of the Stewarts. Although ruinous it has many fine architectural and design features. It is also said to have a number of ghostly spirits, including Mary – although not as a baby! One story mentions a female apparition on her knees praying in the chapel, which has been identified by some as Mary.

It is also claimed that there is an apparition of a Blue Lady, that walks from the original entrance of the palace to the nearby parish church of St Michael. Sightings of this phantom are said to occur during mornings of the months of April and September. The rustling sound of a dress has also been heard in the same area.

There is another female spirit claimed to be either Margaret Tudor or Mary of Guise, waiting for the return of their husbands in Queen Margaret's Bower at the top of one of the stair towers. One account described this apparition as a White Lady, accompanied by the smell of perfume. As Margaret Tudor was unhappily married to James IV and Marie of Guise was such a formidable lady and outlived her husband James V by some 18 or so years, neither candidate seems entirely likely.

The apparitions at Linlithgow are those of adult women and Mary certainly visited the palace as an adult. As a Catholic Mary would have prayed in the chapel, but her mother and grandmother had stronger associations with the palace and are as likely candidates for the spirit.

During Mary's early years in Scotland she was moved around the kingdom for safety and stayed at Stirling, Inchmahome Priory and Dumbarton Castle but it is the castles and houses she visited after her return to Scotland in 1561, and particularly after she met Darnley in 1565, that appear to have generated most of the stories.

Although several places were definitely visited by Mary during her many progresses, some of the claims made about Mary's ghost are vague and lack any justification; that is they lack specific context or reason or any known connection with Mary. An apparition of a woman is said to haunt **Melville Castle**, now replaced by a later mansion. The apparition walked through a wall, later revealed to be a blocked-up doorway, and voices and other noises have also been reported. The apparition was witnessed during renovation work. However a more plausible explanation is that the spirit is that of Elizabeth Rennie, wife of Henry Dundas, 1st Viscount Melville. Melville married Elizabeth when she was 14 years old and Melville gained much of his wealth and property through the marriage. Elizabeth, however, committed

Melville Castle

adultery and confessed her misdemeanour to her husband. The couple were subsequently divorced, Dundas keeping the money, property and children. One account suggests that Elizabeth never saw her children again, in which case perhaps the spirit is Elizabeth, searching for her children? Elizabeth died in 1847, having outlived her husband.

Mary may have visited **Dalkeith House** or Palace, also in Midlothian; the building certainly witnessed a number of key events and people during its long history so it is likely she stayed here at some point. Margaret Tudor met James IV at the castle; Cardinal David Beaton was imprisoned here; the English took the castle in 1547 after the Battle of Pinkie; General Monck, Cromwell's commander in Scotland, was based at the castle, and several later monarchs also visited. Students from the University of Wisconsin in the US live in the house during a study abroad programme and some of them have witnessed a number of manifestations: one student claimed that she saw a female figure holding her head under her arm, at the foot of her bed, which was later claimed to have been Mary.

Other occurrences include unexplained footsteps, voices, laughter and moving light balls. There is allegedly a Green Lady and/or a young girl called Anna who, when she was about eight, fell out of an upper window. It has been suggested that the disturbances may be caused by the ghosts of Anna and her nursemaid or the Green Lady – or perhaps Mary.

Dalkeith House (see previous page)

Falkland Palace is another royal residence of the Stewarts and Mary visited several times, including in 1563. Falkland was used as a hunting lodge and remodelled by James III, James IV and James V. The tapestry gallery is said to be haunted by a White or Grey Lady, an anonymous woman, who died of a broken heart waiting for the return of her lover from battle. The apparition walks along the gallery and disappears through a wall where previously there was a door. It is claimed that this apparition is that of Mary in one account, but more usually the identity is not known.

In the **Covenanter Hotel** on the High Street in Falkland, directly opposite the palace, several manifestations have been reported. These include sudden drop in temperature, smell of lavender, and strange noises and footsteps, associated with two of the bedrooms, as well as the apparition of a woman identified as Mary gliding about a bedroom, even though the present building dates from after her death. Again there is no other indication that this activity has anything to do with Mary and theories suggested by paranormal investigators include the spirit of a French woman looking out the window and even that of Sir George 'Bluidy' MacKenzie, the judge responsible for ordering the imprisonment, torture and execution of Covenanters. He is said to have stayed here when it was called the Commercial Inn, which is possible. Incidentally the much maligned MacKenzie also

Covenanter Hotel, Falkland

allegedly haunts Greyfriars Kirkyard in Edinburgh, where a number of Covenanters were held in captivity and many manifestations have been reported there.

Glamis Castle in Angus is reputedly one of the most haunted castles in Scotland. It is an impressive building consisting of an original 14th-century keep with many later additions. Mary visited here in 1562, some time before the confrontation with the Earl of Huntly at Corrichie, but although it is claimed several apparitions and manifestations occur at the castle none of them are said to be Mary.

A male known as 'Earl Beardie' who may have been either Alexander Lyon, 2nd Lord Glamis, or Alexander Lindsay, 4th Earl of Crawford, is said to have played cards with the devil on a Sunday, a double sin, and as a result is doomed to play forever in a sealed up room, from where swearing and the rattling of dice could be heard.

Lady Janet Douglas, sister of the 5th Earl of Angus, was married to John Lyon, 6th Lord Glamis. James V (Mary's father) had a long campaign of revenge against the Douglas Earl of Angus, and Lady Janet was accused of treason by supporting her brother, a baseless charge of murdering her husband by poison and, finally, of even using witchcraft. She was executed by being burnt at Castle Hill in Edinburgh in 1537 and her apparition, a Grey or

White Lady, is said to haunt Glamis, and has been seen in the chapel and the clock tower. There are also stories that she haunts the esplanade at Edinburgh Castle where she was executed.

Tales also circulate of ghostly animals, giants, sounds of gallows being constructed, as well as allegedly the spirit of a little African boy, none of which have any particular explanation. One claim about this last story is that the wee boy was a servant of Mary, but on what evidence is uncertain.

Mary also visited **Doune Castle**, near Stirling, occasionally, and it was held until 1570 by forces loyal to her. One report alleges that light balls have been witnessed which are claimed to be manifestations of Mary's spirit. However the account also states that Mary was exiled here, which is totally inaccurate, and that the apparition of her wore a 'blood velvet gown'. Doune was a dower house used by Mary of Gueldres, widow of James II; Margaret of Denmark, widow of James III; and Margaret Tudor, widow of James IV, but Mary was never imprisoned or exiled here. Doune Castle was used to film several scenes in *Monty Python and the Holy Grail* and also featured in *Ivanhoe* with Elizabeth Taylor and Robert Taylor in 1952 and more recently was used as the set for Winterfell in the TV series *Game of Thrones*.

Mary is claimed to be associated with the reputed hauntings of **Houndwood House** in the Borders. She did visit the 16th-century tower house in 1565 and some unspecific ghostly manifestations have been linked to her and the finding of her ring. The house is also said to be haunted by other apparitions and manifestations: Chappie the apparition of the lower part of a man, dressed in riding breeches, was witnessed in the grounds outside the house in the 19th century. Sounds of heavy footsteps, knocking, rapping and horses have also reported.

Eilean Donan Castle, near Dornie, allegedly has a female ghost called Lady Mary who is said to haunt one of the bedrooms, and which, in at least one report, has been identified as Mary Queen of Scots. It is just possible that Mary visited here during one of her royal progresses, perhaps when she visited the northeast in 1563, but there is no record of a visit. The Lady Mary ghost is some other female associated with the castle. The site is also said to be haunted by the ghost of a Spanish soldier, who was killed when the castle was attacked during the 1719 Jacobite Rising.

As an adult, Mary visited many other locations that are associated with very specific, often dramatic, events in her life. She visited **Rossend Castle** in Fife in February 1563 when the young French poet Chastelard forced his way into the queen's bedchamber. He had previously hidden under her bed at Holyroodhouse and had been ordered to leave her household, which order had clearly been ignored. Chastelard was executed at St Andrews and

Eilean Donan Castle (see previous page)

the chamber, used by Mary, is said to be haunted by a somewhat vague 'ghost'. No detailed descriptions of the manifestation have been recorded and there are no claims that it is Mary's spirit.

Mary and Darnley first met at **Wemyss Castle**, also in Fife, in 1565. The castle belonged to the Wemyss family and they supported her at Langside. A Green Lady allegedly haunts the restored castle; reports claim that she has been seen in several areas and rooms. The figure – given the name Green Jean – was seen in the 1890s and described as being tall and slim and wearing a long green gown, hiding her face with a hood. In 1905 a family member reported a similar apparition and noted that the material of her dress made a swishing or rustling sound. There is no suggestion this a ghost of Mary.

The **Palace of Holyroodhouse** in Edinburgh was the site of another violent event during the dramatic years between her marriage to Darnley and her abdication. Darnley and other conspirators murdered Mary's Italian secretary and musician, David Rizzio, in front of the pregnant queen in her private chambers in March 1566. A blood stain on the floor allegedly cannot be washed off and, perhaps not surprisingly, Rizzio's ghost is said by some to haunt the palace. It is claimed that Mary's spirit has also been witnessed here but there are no details of any sightings; however there are at least two other female spirits at Holyroodhouse. One is a Grey Lady who is thought to have been one of Mary's companions or member of her household: her apparition and footsteps have been witnessed in the queen's audience chamber. A naked female ghost has also been reported roaming the palace and gardens. It has been given the name Bald Agnes, thought to be the spirit of Agnes Sampson who was one of the many people accused in the North Berwick witch trials during the reign of James VI. Agnes was found guilty and executed in 1591.

Before moving to the safety of Edinburgh Castle after the murder, Mary and Darnley journeyed to **Dunbar Castle**, in East Lothian. Bothwell also brought her here the following year, allegedly by force, before they married. Although the castle ruins are said to be haunted, it is a ghost known as Black Aggie who has been reportedly seen on clear nights, not Mary. Black Agnes, Countess of Dunbar, and daughter of Sir Thomas Randolph, held the castle for six weeks in 1388 against the English, who were forced to withdraw their attack. Agnes survived and lived into her sixties. Her husband, Patrick, the 9th Earl of Dunbar, is also said to haunt the site and other manifestations include the sound of ghostly bagpipes – although that may be the sound of waves rolling in the caves or even a local piper getting in some practice.

Edinburgh Castle has a whole host of different ghosts and manifestations: piper, drummer, prisoners, dogs, and light balls. The spectral figure of Lady Janet Douglas, who allegedly haunts Glamis Castle, is also said to have been seen on the esplanade at Edinburgh. Edinburgh Castle saw much military action during the Wars of Independence and, as an important stronghold, was held for Mary until 1573. In 1566, Mary gave birth to her son in the palace block after the dramatic murder of Rizzio at Holyroodhouse, but there is only one vague reference to Mary's ghost haunting the castle. Mary was allegedly helped in the birth by the presence of St Margaret's girdle, the relic being brought from Dunfermline. St Margaret was married to the 11th-century Malcolm Canmore – Malcolm III, King of Scots – and had many successful pregnancies.

Mary and Darnley, and possibly the infant Prince James, visited **Traquair House**, south of Innerleithen in the Borders. The house incorporates some 12th-century work but was remodelled in the 15th, 16th and 17th centuries. Mary and Darnley enjoyed a hunting trip here and she left behind a quilt as a gift; it is claimed that she and her Four Marys embroidered it. The 4th Laird also helped with Mary's escape from Lochleven and the bed on which she slept at Terregles Castle, during her last days and nights in Scotland, is at the house. However, despite being reputedly the oldest, continuously inhabited house in Scotland, Traquair House does not appear to be haunted by Mary or any other spirits. An apparition, allegedly that of Lady Louisa Stewart, who died in 1875 when she was nearly 100 years old, has been reported to have been seen walking by the Quair burn in the grounds, but not in the house.

In October 1566 Mary visited **Hermitage Castle**, following the birth of Prince James. The Earl of Bothwell who, by 1566, had developed a close relationship with the queen, held the strong, oppressive castle located in the Borders. He was Mary's lieutenant in the Border Marches and had been

Hermitage Castle

badly injured during a skirmish with Wee Jock Elliot of Park. Elliot later died from wounds suffered in the encounter. Mary rode to Hermitage to visit Bothwell and, due to the length of the ride and falling from her horse, suffered a serious episode of ill health afterwards. It is this fact that has been used to claim that the White Lady witnessed outside the castle at Hermitage might be Mary – however it would make more sense that she would haunt

Jedburgh where she lay on, what was thought by many to be, her deathbed.

Other spectres allegedly haunt Hermitage: the cries and screams of the victims of a Lord Soulis who owned the property in the 14th century. It is said that Soulis kidnapped local children to use in his diabolic rituals. Legend records that Soulis was then wrapped in lead and boiled in a cauldron at a stone circle. Whatever the truth of his demise, the family were forfeited in 1320. Soulis himself is said to haunt the castle, but another story involves Sir Alexander Ramsay who was taken prisoner by the Knight of Liddesdale, William Douglas, in 1338. Ramsay was held in the dungeon prison at the castle and starved to death and the sounds of his screams and cries for help have been reported.

After Mary visited Bothwell at Hermitage, she returned to a 16th-century town house in Jedburgh, now known as **Mary Queen of Scots House**; it belonged to the Scotts of Ancrum and later the Kerrs. Mary lay, seriously ill, for a month in a chamber on the second floor. Her companions, the Four Marys, are said to have used the chamber above. A version of Mary's death mask is housed in the museum here and there have been reports from visitors that they have heard rustling sounds and smelled the scent of freesias in the room used by Mary. In 2012, paranormal investigators claimed they communicated with a female spirit called Rosie; they also saw a number of light orbs in the room used as a picture gallery.

Stirling Castle is claimed to be haunted by Mary. Several important events in Mary's life happened at Stirling: she was crowned in the old chapel in 1543, returned several times during her travels around Scotland, and had

Stirling Castle

her son baptised here in 1566. The Catholic baptism at Stirling has been seen as Mary's moment of triumph and glory; soon followed by a rapid descent into disaster. Nevertheless it was a key event, took more planning than her marriages to either Darnley or Bothwell, and was the only time she requested taxation from her subjects. The castle has a number of alleged spirits including a Pink Lady and a Green Lady.

The Pink Lady is said to be the apparition of a beautiful woman and so some have suggested it might be Mary. Other, more established, accounts suggest that it may be the ghost of a woman searching for her husband who was killed during the siege of the castle by Edward I in 1303. The style of dress worn by Mary in the 16th century would be very different to that worn in the early 14th century; however presumably the spectre was too indistinct to be able to identity such specific detail. This ghost has also been reported in the graveyard of the Church of the Holy Rude, where she is sometimes witnessed at Ladies' Rock between the church and castle.

The Green Lady of Stirling Castle is thought to appear as a harbinger of bad news, particularly fire, and has been seen in recent times, including once in the kitchens. Harbingers and green spirits associated with a particular place are quite common in folk tales and legends, but interpretations have tried to link the spirit with Mary by claiming she might have been one of Mary's ladies or attendants. It is recorded that one of Mary's ladies did report a fire in her bedchamber during one of her visits to the castle. Another account suggests that the Green Lady is the spirit of a daughter of a governor of the castle who fell in love with a soldier, and who then rather dramatically, fell to her death from the highest part of the castle rock, again a frequent motif in ghost stories, a falling.

There are also other manifestations at Stirling. In 1946 and 1956, and again quite recently, footsteps have been heard in a room in the Governor's Block. Stirling also allegedly has a male ghost, known as the Highland Ghost as it is claimed it wears a kilt. The spectre was seen in 1952 by two sentries who said they saw it go from the Douglas Gardens, move along the wall of the King's Old Building and disappear at the tower end. Again this apparition has reportedly been witnessed in recent years, when the castle was undergoing major renovation work on the Great Hall.

Craigmillar Castle in Edinburgh is another location that Mary visited frequently and which is reputedly haunted by a Green Lady, identified by some as Mary. Craigmillar is a strong, imposing and well-preserved ruin, owned by the Preston family who were long-term supporters of Mary. Mary visited here several times, once after Rizzio's murder in 1566. It was, more importantly, the location of a meeting of Mary's privy council later the same

Craigmillar Castle

year. Those who attended included Moray and Maitland of Lethington and later it would be claimed that, with Mary's consent, the murder of Darnley was planned here. There have been reports of a strong smell of lavender in the great hall and some reports of the Green Lady. In 1813 a walled-up skeleton, standing upright, was discovered in one of the vaults. Incidentally, the area around Drummond Street and Old College in Edinburgh, where **Kirk o' Field** was located and where Darnley's murder took place, is allegedly haunted by his ghost, but not by Mary's.

Before marrying in May 1567, Mary and Bothwell stayed at **Hailes Castle**, near East Linton in East Lothian, which belonged to the Hepburns at that time. There are no specific reports that Mary haunts the site, but it is claimed that a White Lady has been seen at the entrance to the castle and the spirit of an imprisoned man, who was starved to death, allegedly haunts one of the two pit prisons. After their hasty marriage, Mary and Bothwell spent some time at **Borthwick Castle** in Midlothian. The castle was built in 1430 and is an imposing fortress with thick walls and a tall twin-towered keep. Mary had previously visited the castle in 1563, under peaceful and happier circumstances, but her final visit was the beginning of the end of her personal reign. The Confederate Lords had gathered their forces and marched to Borthwick, and Mary and Bothwell had to flee the castle; Mary left disguised as a male pageboy. There are several reported apparitions associated with Borthwick, and, perhaps not surprisingly, it is claimed Mary's ghost, in male apparel, appears around the grounds between the castle and the church. It is also claimed that she has been seen in a stairwell near a room that was subsequently called the Mary Queen of Scots' room when the castle was a hotel. Borthwick also boasts another female ghost – Anne Grant – who apparently fell pregnant by one of the Borthwick lords. Heavily pregnant, Anne was slashed across her stomach and both she and her unborn baby died in one of the rooms. Ghostly manifestations have included: a sudden drop in temperature, strange scratching sounds, footsteps, opening of heavy doors and weeping sounds. Another ghost, this time male, is said to have been a servant of the family who was burnt to death after being found to have embezzled money. The sounds of children playing – when there are no children present – have also been reported, although there is no explanation about what that might signify.

Located on a small island, **Lochleven Castle** is a small 15th-century tower surrounded by a 14th-century courtyard. It is perhaps not surprising that Mary's ghost allegedly haunts the castle near Kinross, as it was here that she was imprisoned by her Scottish nobles in 1567, forced by her half-brother

Niddry Castle (see next page)

to sign her abdication, and, most agree, suffered a miscarriage of twins – however reports about the ghostly spirit that haunts the castle are quite vague. The ghost allegedly appears to be looking for something. If it is Mary, perhaps her spirit is searching for her lost babies?

Before travelling to Dumbarton, from where she hoped to sail to France, Mary spent at night at **Niddry Castle**, near Winchburgh, owned by the Setons who were loyal supporters. From here she moved to **Cadzow Castle** in Hamilton, the main seat of the Hamiltons. However, despite the fact that emotions must have been high at this point, Mary's spirit does not appear to haunt either site.

The Hamiltons were strong supporters of Mary and it is claimed, although not confirmed, that she spent time at **Craignethan Castle**, near Lanark, which was a Hamilton property. The spectre of a headless woman in white, which has been identified as Mary, has reportedly been seen in the outer courtyard of the castle. This is, of course, problematic: how can a headless ghost be identified and Mary was definitely not executed in a white gown…

There are also reports of other manifestations in the area that now contains the tearoom and toilets, including pipe music and voices.

However, it also is claimed that Mary may have stayed at either **Castlemilk**, a tower house that was replaced by a mansion, or **Cathcart Castle**, the night before the battle of Langside. Very little remains of the castle and later mansion at Castlemilk, as this has been almost completely demolished, except for the stable block. There were reports that the house and grounds were haunted by a variety of spectral apparitions. These include a Green Lady; a White Lady on a bridge over the burn; and a 'Mad Major' who galloped up to the house at night. It was claimed that this was the ghost of Captain William Stirling Stuart returning from Waterloo. The ruins of Cathcart Castle were reduced to the foundations in the 1980s, and there are no reports of any ghostly activity at this site.

Instead of setting sail from Dumbarton, Mary ordered her forces to attack Regent Moray and his men, who were camped near Glasgow. The ensuing battle at **Langside** on 13 May 1568 was a disaster for Mary, who watched the mêlée from near Cathcart Castle: around 300 of Mary's supporters were killed and some hundreds more taken prisoner; a monument marking the site of the main battle was erected in 1887. Mary herself does not appear to haunt the site but there are reports that ghostly solders appear around what is now a boating pond in Queen's Park at Langside, on the anniversary of the battle. Reports about sightings were recorded in the 1830s and more recently, in 1993, a girl from Glasgow and some friends headed towards the monument after a night on the town. Around midnight, it is said, a mist rose up around the pond and she witnessed apparitions of soldiers fighting each other; the vision lasted around 20 minutes. It is recorded that at least some of the witnesses may have been under the influence of alcohol at the time.

After the battle Mary went to **Cessnock Castle**, near Galston in Ayrshire, and one of her ladies died at the castle. It is claimed that the spirit of Mary's servant haunts the castle. In an interesting twist of dramatic irony, John Knox is also said to haunt the castle, having been heard quoting Protestant scripture.

Mary's last night in Scotland (15/16 May) is thought to have been at **Dundrennan Abbey** near Kirkcudbright. Dundrennan was a Cistercian abbey founded by David I in 1142, and the lay commendator who was appointed in 1562 was Edward Maxwell of Terregles. The Maxwells were Catholic and Mary had already stayed at their castle, Terregles, west of Dumfries, the previous night. The abbey was eventually dissolved, although part was used as a Protestant parish church until 1742. Neither Dundrennan nor Terregles have reports of any ghostly activity related to Mary.

MARY'S GHOSTS IN ENGLAND

Once Mary left Scotland she spent her first night at **Workington Hall** in Cumbria. Also known as Curwen Hall, this ruined fortified manor house was the home of Sir Henry Curwen (a later descendant would join the Jacobite cause). Mary wrote a letter to Elizabeth while at Workington and gave the family an agate cup – the Luck of Workington – which then developed a reputation as a family talisman: as long as it remained unbroken the family would have good luck. 'Galloping Henry', the Jacobite-supporting Curwen, was murdered here by a thief and is said to haunt the hall. Loud thumping noises have been heard and his spectre is said to ride a phantom horse though the building. Mary herself does not appear to haunt Workington.

From Workington, she was then escorted to Carlisle, where vague sightings of her ghostly presence have been reported. **Carlisle Castle** was involved in many battles over the centuries, and there are examples of 'licking stones' in the dungeons, stones that have been licked clean by prisoners trying to suck moisture out of the walls. Perhaps the ghostly spirits are those of the many prisoners who did not survive their captivity rather than Mary? There are, however, vague stories of her ghost haunting the castle, as well in Long Lane, where apparently her phantom was once seen. Another tale is that of the phantom of a woman that a soldier tried to bayonet and then passed out with fear, and that of a small boy.

Mary arrived at **Bolton Castle**, near Wensleydale in Yorkshire, on 15 July 1568; by this time she was being held in custody – for her safety – rather than as a guest. Bolton Castle is an impressive and well-preserved castle built by the Scrope family.

Claims have been made that an apparition wearing a black velvet gown, which has been witnessed in the courtyard, might be Mary.

The current Lord Bolton, a former caretaker, and a lady in the village, have all seen a phantom, perhaps the same one as the descriptions are similar. This apparition is described as woman in a dark coat or cloak, wearing a blouse with a lace collar. Female ghosts in castles are, however, commonplace and this bogle may have no connection with Mary.

Theories about why Mary's spirit might haunt particular places are numerous but her perception of her future must have changed dramatically – and not for the better – at Bolton. She was now held in captivity; she was further away from possible rescue from her Scottish supporters; and the York–Westminster inquiry did not find in her favour. The circumstances

Bolton Castle

surrounding the death of Darnley were declared unsatisfactory and Mary was not cleared of any involvement in it. This must have been a harsh blow and Elizabeth's refusal to meet her must also have disappointed. Maybe this is why Mary's spirit remains here? Although this could be the ghost of another woman.

There are reports of other apparitions and manifestations at Bolton: during a paranormal investigation a medium claimed to see three men in a room surrounded by silver plate and other luxuries; she claimed she could tell the men were plotting a crime. The room that she was in has been known as the Armoury for many generations but originally was a strong room used to store valuables rather than weapons. Other accounts include the sound of drumming from the courtyard and, after staff reassembled a four-poster bed, which is a combination of 18th and 19th-century parts, and put it in the Mary Queen of Scots' chamber, the owners' dogs started barking and snarling at the bed. The bed already had a reputation for giving sleepers nightmares.

Mary's phantom has also been reported at the nearby **Nappa Hall**. She spent some days here during her time at Bolton and allegedly a beautiful female figure wearing a black velvet gown has been seen here – although, as with many of the descriptions of Mary's ghost, the Nappa Hall ghost bears a remarkable similarity to the Hilliard miniature. One recorded sighting was in 1878. A young girl was playing with a small child in the poorly-lit Great Hall when a female figure entered the hall from the far end and walked towards the dais. The girl ran after her and pulled at her gown, but she noticed that the dress was not Victorian in style. The woman then disappeared through a door that led to a turnpike stair. When the young girl later saw a portrait of Mary, she identified the beautiful apparition as her. It might be wondered: did the girl really not see a picture of Mary before her alleged 'appearance'?

From Bolton Mary was moved to the much hated **Tutbury Castle** near Burton-on-Trent. The castle is now largely ruined but even in the 16th century it was already in a poor condition. The apparition of Mary that has allegedly been seen here wears both black and white gowns. A white figure was witnessed around midnight by a group of 40 members of the armed services at the top of the South Tower as recently as 2004. They thought that someone was joking with them but none of the re-enactors were dressed in white. This is an unusual case of a multiple sighting of a possible phantom.

A figure in black has been seen, by members of the custodial staff, between 10.00 and 11.00 pm, standing in the window of the Great Hall, and also witnessed, by archaeologists, walking across a grassed area. Certainly records clearly show that Mary hated this location and was often ill, suffering from her recurrent digestive or rheumatic problems. Two of her personal priests were found dead at Tutbury, and not from natural causes: one was discovered hanged from her window and another one's body was found in a castle well. At one point Mary was so distressed, it was said she ran barefoot and screaming into the snow. It was also during one of her later spells here that the coded letters about the Babington Plot were exchanged, which final, desperate, scheme contributed to her ultimate execution. Perhaps her extreme unhappiness has seeped into the fabric of the castle?

Wingfield Manor in Derbyshire, one of Bess of Hardwick's properties, was also used to hold Mary on several occasions in 1569, 1584 and 1585 and was much more comfortable than either Tutbury or Bolton. Mary was housed in the north-east tower which had views overlooking the valley. Although she was still in custody, the Earl of Shrewsbury and his wife Bess, were not Mary's harshest jailors and she spent many hours with Bess sewing and talking. The site is reputedly haunted by her spirit in the form of balls of light that float around the ruins, particularly in an area referred to as the ballroom, although presumably this was a later designation. Mary may also have been taken to Heage Hall in Derbyshire during these years. It is alleged that an apparition riding a brown horse has been seen, or more often heard, which has, for some reason, been identified as Mary.

Bess of Hardwick and her second husband, Sir William Cavendish, built **Chatsworth House** around 1552. Cavendish died in 1557 and Bess married twice more: Sir William St Loe and then George Talbot in 1567. Ultimately Bess became jealous of the apparently sympathetic relationship that developed between Mary and Shrewsbury, and resented the spiralling costs of providing for their royal prisoner and her staff. Mary was held in the east side of Chatsworth; the rooms are still called the Queen of Scots' Apartments. There are reports of a number of manifestations, not all of which are identified as Mary. Some claim it is the ghost of Bess herself who haunts the house or the spirit of Evelyn, the wife of Victor, 9th Duke of Devonshire, who spent many years restoring rare tapestries and embroideries. Doors opening and closing, footsteps, voices and laughter, thumps and bumps have also been recorded in the corridors and various rooms, including the library.

Very little remains of the main house at **Manor Lodge** in Sheffield, now

Turret House, Manor Lodge, Sheffield

surrounded by a 20th-century housing estate, apart from the Turret House. It was a property of Shrewsbury who remodelled the medieval hunting lodge into a grand manor house. Mary stayed here often during her captivity and, according to local legend, her 'beautiful' spirit, wearing a black gown, has been witnessed walking through walls. Caretakers of the building reported seeing the phantom in the 1930s and there are later accounts of people staying overnight being spooked by some presence and dogs would whimper if left alone. One strange legend is that an imp-shaped incense burner was kept in the top floor to keep away 'evil spirits'. One night, loud banging woke the occupants; they checked the building but did not find anything obviously wrong. However, they chalked a circle around the burner and the next morning discovered the burner outside the circle – nobody admitted to having moved it.

During the Northern Rising in 1569, Mary was sent to Coventry – literally not metaphorically. She spent some time at **St Mary's Guildhall**, situated across from the cathedral. The guildhall was used to hold meetings of Coventry's different guilds, and Henry VI held court here during the Wars of the Roses. The building is popular with ghost hunters and guides have reported a number of strange phenomena: doors opening by themselves; voices coming from empty rooms, and a sensation of being passed by something (or someone) on the stairs. Although the hall apparently houses a variety of spectral manifestations, none of them are claimed to be specifically Mary.

From 1573 Mary was permitted to visit Buxton in Derbyshire several times. Here she stayed at what is now the **Old Hall Hotel**. Shrewsbury and Bess built the building, known as the New Hall, in 1573, on the site of an older inn – the Auld Hall – to provide accommodation for Mary. Here she took the waters and seems to have had regular visits from members of the English nobility. A couplet has been scratched onto the glass pane of the window in what is now Room 26. The original 16th-century building still stands behind a later 17th-century edifice and extension. Some people have claimed that they have felt Mary's presence in Room 26, although there do not appear to be any specific descriptions or sightings of her apparition; perhaps because her time here was relatively comfortable and pleasant?

In 1585 Mary was returned to Tutbury, but she also spent some time at **Chartley Manor Hall** in Staffordshire, property of the Devereux family, before being moved finally to Fotheringhay on 25 September 1586. Chartley Castle was abandoned around 1485 and the Devereux family moved to the nearby moated timber manor house, which was destroyed by fire in 1781. Robert Devereux, 2nd Earl of Essex, was a favourite of Elizabeth at that time – ultimately he would himself be executed for treason in 1601 – and married to Frances Walsingham, daughter of Sir Francis Walsingham, Elizabeth's spymaster. It was during her time at Chartley that Mary first got inveigled in the Babington Plot, which scheming contributed to her trial and death sentence; it may not be that surprising that there are claims that her spirit haunts the area by the manor house, now occupied by a later house. It was from here that she was arrested while out on a hunt as her rooms were being searched for incriminating evidence. However, there are also claims of ghostly sightings at and near the site of the castle ruins, where she did not stay. Some years ago, two teenage girls claimed they witnessed a figure of a woman with orange hair and a pale face in a reddish-pink dress with lace collar and cuffs near the castle. After some research, they decided the figure they had seen was Mary in her red underskirt that she wore on the day of her execution. The sighting was also said to be on the anniversary of her death.

From Chartley Mary was moved to **Tixall Hall**, also in Staffordshire, which was a property of Sir Walter Aston. His father built the hall and Sir Walter built the Gatehouse around 1580. The hall is gone but the gatehouse survives and has been remodelled. It is claimed that the gatehouse has a ghost and that it might be Mary, but there are no descriptions or details of any manifestations.

Haycock Hotel, Wansford (see next page)

The **Haycock Hotel** in Wansford, near Peterborough, was a coaching inn at which Mary may have stayed on her way to her trial at Fotheringhay. The present building dates from 1620; however some guests have reported seeing figures in various public areas in the oldest part of the hotel. There have also been reports of guests feeling that someone or thing was the room with them, and some claim that Mary's apparition has been seen here.

Virtually nothing survives of **Fotheringhay Castle**, a large motte and bailey castle in Northamptonshire, except the earthworks of the motte and a chunk of masonry. The castle was a favourite residence of the house of York and Richard III was born here, but records indicate that it was abandoned and fell into a ruinous state not long after Mary's execution. It was ultimately demolished – possibly on the orders of James VI (and I), although perhaps later. It was thought that the parish church of Fotheringhay housed a carved wooden chair upon which Mary sat immediately before her death, but it seems that it may have been moved to another church at Conington about five miles south of Peterborough.

Perhaps surprisingly, there are no claims that the site of Fotheringhay Castle is haunted by Mary's spirit; however the **Talbot Hotel** at Oundle was built using materials from the castle, in particular windows and the oak staircase. It is alleged that Mary walked down these stairs to her place of execution and her ghostly spirit, wearing her ubiquitous black gown, reputedly haunts the hotel. It is also claimed that an apparition of a gaunt woman has been seen staring out of a window, pictures have been moved, and one guest was woken by the feeling of 'something or someone' sitting on the bed. Most of the activity has allegedly occurred in February, the month of her execution.

It was not until July 1587 that Mary's body was interred at **Peterborough Cathedral**. A former Benedictine monastery, the cathedral is also the burial place of Catherine of Aragon, Henry VIII's first wife. Several ghostly manifestations allegedly haunt the cathedral; however it is not Mary's spirit that lingers here. Sightings of figures, in monastic clothing, have reportedly been seen in the graveyard. Also a male apparition has been identified as a stonemason – perhaps he died during the construction of the cathedral, presumably something that happened fairly often? Another ghost is said to be that of a young girl who was apparently murdered at the cathedral in the 1860s; her spirit has been seen at a window in the precinct buildings. There have also been reports of the sound of singing, when no choir was present, and light balls have been seen floating around the upper floors.

There are also claims that Mary's ghost is one of the many reportedly seen at the **Tower of London**. Given the grisly events it witnessed and the many important people who were imprisoned here, it is not surprising that the Tower is claimed to be haunted: Anne Boleyn's ghost is reported to have been seen at several places around the complex. Lady Jane Grey, who was declared queen after the death of Edward VI, was imprisoned by Mary Tudor and beheaded here on 12 February 1554, along with her husband, Guilford Dudley. Apparitions of both Lady Jane and her husband have been reported in several areas, notably a female figure was seen on the battlements on 12 February 1957, 403 years after her execution. Catherine Howard was also executed and her ghost is said to haunt the place.

Wailing cries and footsteps were reported to have been heard three times in the Tower, on Christmas Day 1900. According to legend, this was the spirit of Mary Queen of Scots and the sound would herald the death of the monarch: Queen Victoria died afterwards on 22 January 1901. However, Mary was never held at the Tower; her body was not taken there after death; and there are no relics or objects associated with Mary held there, so it seems strange that her spirit would haunt this site – especially when others with at least as much motive were executed here.

SOME OTHER ROYAL GHOSTS

In terms of queenly ghosts, Mary wins hands down, beating Elizabeth, Catherine Howard, Lady Jane Grey and even Anne Boleyn with the number and variety of locations that claim to house her spirit. Elizabeth's spectre appears to have been recorded at only a few places: Bradwell Vale; Tilbury in Essex; Windsor Castle; and Richmond Palace. It is claimed that once a year, ghosts of Elizabeth and her royal party have been seen heading towards Hazelbridge Hall at Bradwell Vale in Derbyshire. Elizabeth addressed her forces at Tilbury Fort in Essex as they prepared to face the Spanish Armada and it is said that one of the many apparitions seen here is that of the queen.

She also allegedly haunts the Royal Library at Windsor Castle. The sounds of her footsteps on floorboards have been heard going across the library and into an inner room, and a figure wearing a black gown and shawl has been witnessed at a window in the Deans' Cloister, which has been identified as Elizabeth. Elizabeth liked Windsor Castle and used it as a centre for the royal court and diplomatic meetings. The appearances of the woman in black have been said to increase during times of war: George VI is reported to have seen the vision during the early days of World War II. A figure standing at a window at Windsor, which has been identified as Anne Boleyn rather than Elizabeth, has also been reported on occasion.

Elizabeth also enjoyed spending time at Richmond Palace, where she participated in hunting. She died here on 24 March 1603. It is said that during her last days, Elizabeth was quite delirious and appeared to be tormented by guilt and memories of some of her actions, particularly the death of Mary. It is claimed that one of her ladies-in-waiting, possibly Elizabeth Southwell, witnessed a vision of Elizabeth walking towards her; when she returned to Elizabeth's side in another room, the queen had died. There have also been more recent reports of the sound of horses' hooves in the courtyard.

The ghostly spectre of Lady Jane Grey, who allegedly haunts the Tower of London, has also been seen at Astley Castle in Warwickshire and Bradgate Hall or House in Leicestershire. Ghosts, which are thought to be Lady Jane and her father, Henry Grey, Duke of Suffolk, have apparently been seen at the restored Astley Castle. Jane, her husband and father were all executed in 1554. Jane's ghost has been seen sitting and reading; a headless apparition, said to be her father, is said to walk around the property. Jane was born at Bradgate in 1537 and spent much of her childhood here. Sightings of her ghost in the ruins and parkland have been reported. One particular report alleges that a ghostly coach, pulled by four headless horses, approaches the house on Christmas Eve.

Catherine Howard, Henry VIII's fifth wife, was executed in 1542 and her ghost is believed to haunt Hampton Court Palace, where she was held in custody accused of adultery. During her house arrest, she attempted to escape and plead with Henry. She was caught and dragged through the gallery, kicking and screaming. The gallery is now known as the Haunted Gallery and visitors have reported strange experiences there: screams; feeling faint; drops in room temperature. In 2001, a group of psychologists attempted to assess the causes of these sensations. Thermal cameras recorded drops in temperature at two spots, caused by entirely natural draughts and air currents. The ghostly figure recorded by the camera at 06.00 hours turned out to be a cleaner!

Not surprisingly perhaps, the queen who comes next to Mary in terms of sightings of ghosts is Anne Boleyn. Her spirit has been reported at several locations where she lived, or was held in captivity, and some of the sightings have featured coaches and headless horses – much like the vision of Lady Jane Grey at Bradgate. Anne's ghost allegedly haunts Bollin Hall in Cheshire, where she may have been born and spent some of her childhood. Her ghost has also been reported at Rochford Hall in Essex, where she also spent some time as a young girl. It is claimed that Henry may have met Anne for the first time, and that they may have conducted their early courtship, here. It is

Hever Castle (see next page)

122

reputed that a headless apparition, dressed in a rich silk gown, haunts the site for twelve days over the Christmas period. Bickling Hall in Norfolk, is an alternative site for Anne's birth, and it is claimed that her ghostly spirit appears on the anniversary of her death. The ghostly vision allegedly arrives at the hall in a coach pulled by headless horses. The figure is dressed in white and holds her head in her lap. Other reports claim that the spectre enters the hall and walks through the corridors. A similar version has been reported at Hever Castle in Kent; like Rochford this apparition is also allegedly seen at Christmas time. It is a strange coincidence, or a borrowing from, or conflation of, stories, that both Anne's and Lady Jane Grey's ghostly carriages appear to be more active around Christmas.

Anne's ghost has also been reportedly seen at Hampton Court, wearing a dark gown of blue or black. Some accounts have described the apparition as headless, but others have claimed that the phantom, complete with head, walks slowly and appears very sad. Her apartments here, known as Anne Boleyn's Gate, were incomplete when she was executed. Anne was also held in captivity at Durham House, in Durham House Street in London. The house is no longer in existence but the basement has survived and it is claimed that Anne's ghost haunts the site. Anne was taken to the Tower by barge from Lambeth Palace, and reports claim that her ghost has been witnessed being taken up the river on a ghostly boat. Sounds of her pleading and crying have been reported in the palace itself.

Anne was executed at the Tower on 19 May 1536. Reports of her ghost have been seen at a number of sites here: the White Tower; the Queen's House, where she may have stayed before her coronation; and at the site of her execution, Tower Green. In 1817 a guard suffered a fatal heart attack after allegedly meeting her ghost on the stairs. Another guard used a novel defence during his court martial in 1864. He was found asleep on duty but claimed he had swooned after seeing the figure of a woman in white 'with a queer-looking bonnet with no head in it.' Several other witnesses also claimed they had seen similar visions of a woman in white the same night. The guard also said he had thrust his bayonet at the spectre but the shade had walked into the blade and a flash went through his rifle, giving him a burning shock. An officer said he heard the guard and had seen the figure walk through the guard, who was found not guilty. A similar experience was recorded in 1933 when another guard was so scared he fled his post, shouting for help. A slightly strange legend claims that Anne also haunts Marwell Hall in Hampshire, which was a residence of the Seymours. Allegedly her spectre haunts Yew Tree Walk, where Henry VIII and his next wife Jane Seymour may have walked at the time that Anne was being executed.

Anne was buried at the Church of St Peter ad Vincula, which is located within the tower complex, and it is claimed that her ghost haunts the church. Around 1880, a guard on night duty noticed a light coming from inside the church. When he looked through the window he claimed to have seen a procession of people in Elizabethan dress moving up the aisle, led by a figure he recognised as Anne. Some accounts have said that her body was moved to Salle Church in Norfolk, and secretly buried near her Boleyn ancestors. This has never been confirmed and there are no reports of any ghostly activity similar to the Church of St Peter ad Vincula at Salle.

BEATON'S AND BOTHWELL'S BOGLES

Mary and the other queens are not the only figures who haunt multiple sites: the ghostly apparition of Archbishop, later Cardinal David Beaton, who was murdered by Protestants at St Andrews Castle in 1546, has reportedly been seen in a number of places. St Andrews Castle is an obvious site for

St Andrews Castle

Beaton's ghost, although the castle ruins are also apparently haunted by Archbishop John Hamilton, who was hanged at Stirling, and perhaps Archbishop James Sharp who was assassinated on Magus Moor in 1679. Being an Archbishop in Scotland was no guarantee of a long life…

There is also a White Lady who has been reportedly been seen at the castle and on the beach, but it does not appear that it is Mary's spirit!

Melgund Castle, near Brechin in Angus, was built by Beaton in the 16th century and used by his long-term mistress, Margaret Ogilvie. His ghost has apparently been seen at the ruins of the castle. Ethie Castle, north of Arbroath also in Angus, was another property used by Beaton when he was Abbot of Arbroath; it has been restored and is still inhabited. Ethie is said to be haunted by Beaton's ghostly apparition, first witnessed here shortly after his murder; sounds of footsteps climbing a turnpike stair have also been reported with a dragging noise, suggesting perhaps that Beaton had gout. Some claim that

Ethie was used to hide treasures and valuables from Arbroath Abbey after Beaton was killed. It is also reported that there are other ghostly manifestations at Ethie. The ghost of a child was reported in one of the rooms; when a child's skeleton was found and buried, the manifestations stopped – apparently. Another ghost is a Green Lady, whose appearance is said to herald the death of the owner of the property. It is claimed her apparition has been seen in the walled garden.

Beaton was also said to haunt Balfour House, east of Glenrothes in Fife, now a ruinous mound of rubble. The property passed to the Beaton family around 1360 and they owned it until the end of the 19th century. Mary visited the castle with Darnley but she does not appear to haunt the site. Another place in Fife, Blebo, east of Cupar, is said to have witnessed a manifestation of Beaton. The property was sold to the Beatons, but not until 1649, well after the Cardinal's death. The original castle was abandoned and the family moved to an 18th-century mansion, Blebo House, nearby. However a spectral coach, being driven by a headless coachman, has allegedly been seen on the drive behind the later house, although the occupant has not necessarily been identified as Beaton.

The ghost of Mary's third husband, Bothwell, allegedly haunts Dragsholm Castle in Denmark where he was held in captivity. The castle was used as a prison for noble and ecclesiastical prisoners during the 16th and 17th centuries. At least two other ghosts reportedly seen at the castle are female spirits: a Grey Lady and a White Lady. In keeping with many other similar origin tales, the White Lady is claimed to be the unhappy spirit of a daughter of noble family, possibly Celestine Mariann de Bayonne. Against her father's wishes, the girl fell in love with a man of lower social status and fell pregnant. She was imprisoned in the castle, where her unhappy crying could be heard, and in the early 20th century the skeleton of a young female in a white gown was found in one of the walls. The ghost of a young, woman is said to walk the corridors of the castle. The Grey Lady does not appear to be an unhappy or angry ghost. It is said to be the spirit of a female servant who was helped (some accounts mention that she had been suffering from acute toothache) and supported by the lady of the house and, in thanks, she returns at night to check that everything is in order in the castle.

Bothwell's ghostly spectre is said to ride either into or out of the castle courtyard with his horse and carriage. Other reports mention only the sound of horses' hooves in the yard, with no apparition. Bothwell had hoped to raise an army in support of Mary in Denmark but unfortunately was captured off the coast of Norway and taken to Bergen. This was the home of Anna Throndsen, to whom he had been engaged and possibly married in 1559,

Dragsholm Slot (Castle)

before quickly abandoning her. Anna sued him and as a result he was taken prisoner and held in Dragsholm, ultimately dying insane in 1578. According to legend, Bothwell was tied to a pillar in the dungeon throughout his captivity and fed only minimal food and water. The pillar is still in the castle, and the groove he made on the ground beside it is visible, perhaps more reliable visual evidence of Bothwell's imprisonment and presence than the sound of ghostly horses.

Bothwell was buried nearby at Faarevejle, but he was later disinterred and it was found that his body had been mummified by the sea air. Bizarrely a gruesome portrait was painted in 1861 by Otto Bache, which is now in the National Galleries of Scotland. The mummy was, equally bizarrely, put on display in a museum in Copenhagen, where it was a popular attraction, although Bothwell's remains are now buried in the crypt of the Faarevejle Church. There are displays about him in the building.

MAP OF BRITAIN

ORKNEY

Spynie • Huntly
• Inverness • Delgatie
• Eilean Donan
Corrichie • ABERDEEN
Blairs •
Dunnottar
• Blair • Edzell
DUNDEE • Arbroath
• Balmerino
Stirling • Falkland
Dumbarton EDINBURGH
GLASGOW • Pinkie
Carberry Hill
Langside Jedburgh • BERWICK
Hermitage • Flodden

• Dumfries
Dundrennan •
• CARLISLE
Workington

SEE MAP ON
NEXT PAGE

• Bolton
Nappa

• YORK

SHEFFIELD
Buxton • • Chatsworth
• Wingfield
Chartley • DERBY
STAFFORD • • Tutbury
Tixall
Wansford
Fotheringhay • PETERBOROUGH
Oundle
• COVENTRY

• LONDON

MAP OF SOUTHEAST SCOTLAND

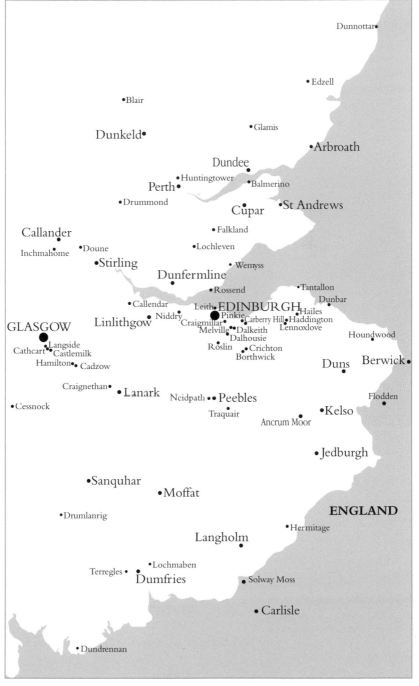

Dunnottar•

• Edzell

•Blair

•Glamis

Dunkeld•

•Arbroath

Dundee

Huntingtower•
Perth•   •Balmerino

•Drummond   •St Andrews

Cupar

•Falkland

Callander   •Lochleven

Inchmahome•   •Doune   • Wenyss
•Stirling

Dunfermline

•Rossend   •Tantallon
•Callendar   Dunbar
Linlithgow   •Niddry   Leith•EDINBURGH   •Hailes
GLASGOW   Craigmillar•Pinkie   •Haddington
Langside   Melville••Dalkeith   Lennoxlove   Carberry Hill
Cathcart••Castlemilk   Roslin•   Dalhousie   Houndwood
Hamilton••   Cadzow   •Crichton
Craignethan•   Borthwick
•Cessnock   •Lanark   Ncidpath ••Peebles   Duns   Berwick•
          Traquair   Flodden
•Sanquhar   Ancrum Moor   •Kelso
•Drumlanrig   •Moffat
Terregles •   •Lochmaben   •Jedburgh
Dumfries
Langholm   ENGLAND
•Dundrennan   •Hermitage
          •Solway Moss
          •Carlisle

129

PLACES TO VISIT

ARBROATH ABBEY
Off A92, Arbroath, Angus. (DD11 1EG)
The substantial ruins of a Tironsenian abbey, founded in 1178 by William the Lyon, in memory of his friend Thomas Becket. Ruins of the church remain, including the fine west end, the gatehouse, sacristy and the Abbot's House, which houses a museum.

Mary visited in 1562 during a progress, staying in the Abbot's House.

This part of the abbey is reputed to be haunted, with knocking and banging being reported from unoccupied areas. The sacristy, which was used as a prison, is also said to be haunted.

Open all year: Apr-Sep, daily 9.30-17.30; Oct-Mar, daily 9.00-16.30; closed 25/26 Dec & 1/2 Jan.

Historic Scotland. Parking. Shop. Refreshments. WC. Admission charge.
Disabled access. Herb garden.
01241 878756. www.historic-scotland.gov.uk

BALMERINO ABBEY
Off A914, 4.5 miles SW of Newport on Tay, Balmerino, Fife. (DD6 8BQ)
In a peaceful setting by the shore of the Firth of Tay are the fragmentary but scenic remains of a 13th-century Cistercian abbey, founded in 1229 by Ermengarde, widow of William the Lyon, and their son Alexander II.

Mary visited in 1565, even though it had been sacked by Reformers, and had dinner in the abbey.

Ermengarde was buried in front of the altar (the site now marked by a wooden cross). Her tomb was despoiled in the 1830s and her bones sold or given away, while her sarcophagus was smashed up.

The ruins of abbey are said to be haunted by a Green Lady, possibly an apparition of Ermengarde. Another story is that the phantom of a robed and hooded man has also been seen here, pushing a wheelbarrow.

Access at all reasonable times.

National Trust for Scotland. Parking. Free entry.
0844 493 2185. www.nts.org.uk

BLAIR CASTLE

Off B8079, 7 miles N of Pitlochry, 1 mile NW of Blair Atholl, Perthshire. (PH18 5TL)
Set in extensive parkland and nestling in a rugged estate of 145,000 acres is the white-washed and castellated Blair Castle, a rambling mansion of the Dukes of Atholl. Blair Castle is the last stronghold in Britain to be besieged, albeit unsuccessfully, having been attacked by the Jacobites in 1746.

Mary visited in 1564 during a progress.

According to one account, the castle is said to have a Grey Lady, who glides about silently.

Open Apr-Oct, daily 9.30-17.30 (last admission 16.30)

Parking. Shop. Restaurant. WC. Disabled access to ground floor & facilities. Admission charged.
Garden.
01796 481207. www.blair-castle.co.uk

BLAIRS MUSEUM

On B9077, 5 miles S of Aberdeen, South Deeside Road, Blairs, Aberdeenshire. (AB12 5YQ)
Formally St Mary's College Blairs, founded in 1829 as a Catholic seminary by local landowner John Menzies of Pitfodels. The seminary closed in 1986 but has subsequently reopened as a museum housing Scotland's Catholic heritage, including textiles, paintings, silver and Jacobite memorabilia as well as portraits of Mary.

Open Apr-Oct, Sat and Sun 14.00-17.00, holiday Mondays 14.00-17.00; other times by arrangement.

Parking. Shop. Refreshments. WC. Disabled access. Admission charged. Chapel.
01224 863767. www.blairsmuseum.com

BOLTON CASTLE

Off A864, 6 miles W of Leyburn, Yorkshire. (DL8 4ET)
In a picturesque spot, Bolton Castle is a large and well-preserved medieval fortress, built by the Scrope family. The building consists of four massive towers, with joining ranges, constructed around a courtyard.

Mary was imprisoned here from 1568.

There are stories of an apparition being seen by three different people, that of a woman in a dark coat or cloak, wearing a blouse with a lace collar. This has been identified by some as Mary's ghost.

Open mid Feb-beg Nov, daily 10.00-17.00 (until 18.00 during summer hols).

Parking. Shop. Cafe. WC. Admission charged. Gardens.
01969 623981. www.boltoncastle.co.uk

BORTHWICK CASTLE

Off A7, 2 miles SE of Gorebridge, Borthwick, Midlothian. (EH23 4QY)
One of the most impressive castles in Scotland, Borthwick Castle is a magnificent looming tower house, rising to 110 feet high with walls up to 14 feet thick. The castle was built by Sir William Borthwick in 1430, whose stone effigy is in nearby Borthwick Church.

Mary and her new husband Bothwell visited the castle in 1567 and were besieged here, Mary only escaping disguised as a man. Mary had also visited during progresses in 1563 and in 1565.

Her ghost is said to have been witnessed here, dressed as a page boy, between the castle and the nearby church, as well as in the castle, in a stair near the Mary Queen of Scots Room when the castle was a hotel.
Castle not open (view from exterior); Borthwick Church open all year, daily.
www.borthwickcastle.com

CADZOW CASTLE

Off A72, 1.5 miles SE of Hamilton, Chatelherault, Lanarkshire. (ML3 7UE)
Standing in Chatelherault park, the present ruin dates from the first half of the 16th century. The castle was long held by the Hamiltons, who were made Earls of Arran and Dukes of Châtelherault in France. In 1579 the castle was captured because of the Hamiltons' continued support for Mary, and then dismantled to be left as a ruin.

Mary visited the castle in 1568 after escaping from Lochleven.

No stories of ghosts have been found.
Park open to the public except Christmas and New Year – castle: view from exterior as fenced off for consolidation work.
Historic Scotland. 01698 426213. www.historic-scotland.gov.uk

CALLENDAR HOUSE

Off A803, Callendar Park, in Falkirk. (FK1 1YR)
Set in a fine public park, Callendar House, a large ornate mansion of the 1870s with towers and turrets, incorporates an old castle. The lands were held by the Livingston family, who were later made Earls of Callendar. Mary Livingston, one of the Four Marys, was from the family

Mary stayed here in 1562 during a progress, as well as in 1565.

One story is that the house is haunted by the ghost of a young woman. During a wedding, a game of hide and seek was played. The girl hid in a trunk in the attic, but was then trapped and suffocated, not being found for three days.
Open all year: Mon–Sat 10.00–17.00; also Apr–Sep, Sun 14.00–17.00; open most public hols; park open all year.
Parking. Shop. Tearoom. WC. Disabled access. Park.
01324 503770. www.falkirkcommunitytrust.org

CARBERRY HILL BATTLE SITE

Off A6124, 2.5 miles SE of Musselburgh, at Carberry Hill. (EH21 8PZ)
The site of the battle on 15 June 1567, which resulted in Mary giving herself up, at Queen Mary's Mount, to the Confederate Lords. Bothwell fled the scene. Although Mary's forces and her enemies faced up to each other there was no actual fighting. There is a monument to the battle (although not apparently that easy to find) with woodland walks in the vicinity.
Access at all reasonable times.

CARLISLE CASTLE

N of Carlisle town centre, Cumbria. (CA3 8UR)
Involved often in the centuries of warfare between England and Scotland, Carlisle Castle is a large, impressive and complex medieval castle. David I died here in 1153.

Mary briefly stayed here after fleeing to England in 1568. There are vague stories of her ghost haunting the castle, as well in Long Lane, where apparently her phantom was once seen.

Open Apr-Oct, daily; Nov-Mar, wknds only.
English Heritage. Parking. Refreshments. Shop. WC. Admission charged. Museum.
01228 591922. www.english-heritage.org.uk

CHARTLEY HALL

Off A518, 0.5 miles NW of Stowe-by-Chartley, Stafford, Staffordshire, England. (ST18 0LN)
Chartley Hall was a large impressive Elizabethan moated manor, but it was demolished after a fire in the 1780s and replaced by a building of 1847. There is the impressive ruin of a 13th-century castle, but it was already ruinous in the 16th century.

At that time Chartley was held by Robert Devereux, 2nd Earl of Essex. In 1575 Elizabeth was entertained at Chartley Hall, and Mary was held prisoner here between December 1585 and September 1586, before she was taken to Fotheringhay Castle.

There are stories that the castle ruin and area are haunted, including by an apparition identified as Mary, described as having very pale skin and orange hair, and clad in a pink dress with lacy cuffs and collar.

CHATSWORTH

Off B6012, Bakewell, Derbyshire, England. (DE45 1PP)
Set in more than 105 acres of gardens, Chatsworth is the magnificent mansion of the Duke of Devonshire, held by 16 generations of the Cavendish family. The house is also home to one of Europe's most significant art collections.

Bess of Hardwick married into the Cavendish family in 1547. Bess was Mary's jailer and Mary was held at Chatsworth several times between 1569 and 1584. Mary's lodgings were on the east side of the house and, although completely refurbished, are still known as the Queen of Scots' Apartments.

Some stories have Mary haunting Chatsworth, although another identity for the ghost is given as Evelyn, wife of the 9th Duke, while a third suggestion is Bess of Hardwick herself.

Open all year, mid March–23 December, daily.
Parking (charge). Restaurants and cafes. Shops. Disabled access. Admission charge. Garden.
01245 565300. www.chatsworth.org

COVENANTER HOTEL, FALKLAND

Off A912, The Square, High Street, Falkland (opposite the Palace), Fife. (KY15 7BU)
The present building, for much of its history known as the Commercial Inn, dates from 1771 but stands on the site of an earlier dwelling. It is now used as a hotel, and is said to be haunted by the apparition of a woman, which has been identified as Mary, seen to glide across a bedroom.

Hotel and restaurant.
01337 857163. www.covenanterfalkland.co.uk

CRAIGMILLAR CASTLE

Off A68, 3 miles SE of Edinburgh Castle, Craigmillar, Edinburgh. (EH16 4SY)

A strong, imposing and well-preserved ruin, Craigmillar Castle consists of a large keep, surrounded by a curtain wall with round corner towers and an outer courtyard. The Prestons held the property from 1374 and were Mary's loyal supporters.

Mary stayed at Craigmillar on several occasions, including in 1563, and fled here after the murder of Rizzio in 1566. It was also at the castle that Moray, Bothwell and William Maitland of Lethington plotted Darnley's murder of 1567.

There are also stories of a Green Lady haunting the vicinity, said by some to be the bogle of Mary.

Open all year: Apr–Sep, daily 9.30–17.30; Oct, daily 9.30–16.30, Nov–Mar, Sat–Wed 9.30–16.30; closed 25/26 Dec and 1/2 Jan.

Historic Scotland. Parking. Shop. WC. Limited disabled access. Admission charged.

0131 661 4445. www.historic-scotland.gov.uk

CRAIGNETHAN CASTLE

Off A72, 4.5 miles W of Lanark, Craignethan, Lanarkshire. (ML11 9PL)

Standing on a promontory above a deep ravine, Craignethan is a ruinous castle, consisting of a strong tower surrounded by a curtain wall on three sides, with a thick rampart on the landward side. It was built as an early castle to withstand artillery, but although attacked and eventually slighted, never withstood a determined siege. The castle was held by the Hamiltons.

Mary may have stayed here before Langside in 1568, although other castles, including Cathcart and Castlemilk, have been suggested.

The castle is said to be haunted by a headless ghost, perhaps the spirit of Mary, as well as other bogles.

Open Apr–Sep, daily 9.30–17.30.

Historic Scotland. Parking. Shop. WC. Admission charged.

01555 860364. www.historic-scotland.gov.uk

CRICHTON CASTLE

Off B6367, 2 miles E of Gorebridge, Crichton, Midlothian. (EH37 5XA)

A complex, large and striking building, Crichton Castle consists of ruinous ranges of buildings enclosing a small courtyard. One particularly fine feature is the arcaded, diamond-faced facade in the courtyard. The castle was a property of the Crichtons, but later passed to the Earls of Bothwell. The former collegiate church is next to the car park.

Mary attended the wedding here of James Stewart, Earl of Moray, her half-brother, in 1562.

The castle is said to be haunted by a horseman, who enters the castle by the original gate, which is now walled up. The ghost of Sir William Crichton is reputed to haunt the ruinous stables.

Castle open Apr–Sep, daily 9.30–17.30 (walk to castle); collegiate church open May–Sep, Sun 14.00–17.00 (01875 320502; www.crichtonchurch.com).

Historic Scotland, Parking (walk to castle 600 yards). Sales area. Admission charged.

01875 320017. www.historic-scotland.gov.uk

Crichton Castle (see previous page)

DALKEITH HOUSE

Off A6094, 0.5 miles NW of Dalkeith, Midlothian. (EH22 2NJ)

In a fine country park, Dalkeith House (or Palace) is an impressive classical mansion, which incorporates part of an old castle, possibly dating from as early as the 12th century. Dalkeith was long held by the Douglases of Morton, and the castle was taken by the English after the Battle of Pinkie in 1547. James Douglas, 4th Earl of Morton, was Chancellor for Mary, and later Regent for the young James VI. James VI visited in 1581, after Morton had been executed. The house is used as a college for students from Wisconsin.

One tale is that the house is haunted by the ghost of Mary, one account being that the apparition appeared headless at the end of one student's bed and then told them to get out. There are other rumours of supernatural manifestations.

Country park open Easter–Oct, daily 10.00–17.00. House not open.

Parking. Tea room. WC. Disabled partial access. Admission charged.

0131 654 1666/0131 663 5684. www.dalkeithcountryestate.com

DELGATIE CASTLE

Off A947, 2 miles E of Turriff, Banff and Buchan, Aberdeenshire. (AB53 5TD)

An imposing and interesting old edifice, Delgatie Castle may incorporate work from the

11th century and was long a property of the Hays. There are fine painted ceilings, dating from 1592 and 1597.

Mary stayed in the castle for three days after the Battle of Corrichie in 1562.

The ghost of a young woman, known as Rohaise, is said to haunt the bedroom off the main stair, which now bears her name. Reputedly, she likes to visit men who stay in the chamber.

Open all year, daily 10.00-17.00; closed for two weeks over Xmas and New Year.

Parking. Gift shop. Tearoom. WC. Disabled access to tearoom and front hall only. Admission charged.

01888 563479. www.delgatiecastle.com

DOUNE CASTLE

Off A820, 7 miles NW of Stirling, SE of Doune, Stirlingshire. (FK16 6EA)

Standing on a strong site in a lovely location, Doune Castle is a powerful courtyard castle with two towers linked by a lower range. The fine Lord's Hall has a carved oak screen, musicians' gallery and a double fireplace. The castle was built by Robert Stewart, Duke of Albany, but passed to the Crown and was used as a dower house.

It was occasionally used by Mary, and was held by forces loyal to her until 1570.

This is another castle she is said to haunt, although evidence is vague,.

Open all year: Apr-Sep, daily 9.30-17.30; Oct, daily 9.30-16.30; Nov-Mar, Sat-Wed 9.30-16.30; closed 25/26 Dec and 1/2 Jan.

Historic Scotland. Parking. Shop. WC. Disabled limited access. Admission charged.

01786 841742. www.historic-scotland.gov.uk

136

DRAGSHOLM SLOT

Dragsholm Alle, 4354 Horve, Denmark.
Dragsholm is magnificent and imposing castle and mansion, which dates from the 12th century. It became a Royal property in the 17th century, and then was held by the Adler family until the 1930s. Now a sumptuous hotel, it was long a feared prison.

Bothwell was imprisoned here on suspicion of the murder of Darnley, apparently chained to a pillar in the cellars. He died here in 1578, and it is said that his ghost haunts the castle, manifestations mostly being of a carriage and horses in the courtyard, although mostly heard rather than seen.

Perhaps more disturbingly, when Bothwell's body was exhumed it was found to be mummified and a gruesome portrait was made of his head. His body was also put on display in a museum in Copenhagen, although it has since been put back in a coffin.

Dragsholm has other ghost stories, including a Grey Lady, who looks after people in the castle, and a White Lady, the bogle of a daughter of the lord walled up in the castle for falling in love with the wrong man.
Hotel.
www.dragsholm-slot.dk

DRUMLANRIG CASTLE

Off A76, 3 miles NW of Thornhill, Drumlanrig, Dumfries and Galloway. (DG3 4AQ)
Set in a fantastic location in 90,000 acres and surrounded by parkland and gardens, Drumlanrig is an impressive 17th-century mansion incorporating older work, consisting of four ranges around a courtyard, with higher rectangular towers at the corners. The property was held by the Douglases, but later passed to the Scott Dukes of Buccleuch. There is a fine art collection.

Mary visited during a progress in 1563.

Three ghosts are said to haunt the castle. One is reputed to be the spirit of Lady Anne Douglas, seen with her head under her arm; another that of a young woman in a flowing dress; and the third of a monkey or other creature, witnessed in the Yellow Monkey Room.
Castle open end Mar-late Aug, daily 11.00 to last tour at 16.00; country park open 10.00-17.00.
Parking. Shop. Tea room. WC. Disabled access. Admission charged. Park land, woodland walks and gardens.
01848 331555. www.drumlanrig.com

DRUMMOND CASTLE GARDENS

Off A822, 2.5 miles SW of Crieff, Drummond, Perthshire. (PH7 4HZ)
Built on a rocky outcrop, Drummond Castle is a fine castle, dating from the 15th century, with splendid gardens. The terraces overlook a magnificent parterre, celebrating the saltire and family heraldry, surrounding a famous sundial by John Milne, Master Mason to Charles I. This was a property of the Drummonds, who were made Earls of Perth, but they later lost the castle after being forfeited following the Jacobite Risings.

Mary visited during a progress in 1567.
Gardens open Easter & May-Oct 13.00-18.00. Castle not open.
Parking. Shop. Disabled partial access. WC. Admission charged.
01764 681433 www.drummondcastlegardens.co.uk

Drummond Castle Gardens (see previous page)

DUMBARTON CASTLE

Off A814, in Dumbarton. (G82 1JJ)

Standing on a commanding rock on the north shore of the Clyde, little remains of the medieval Dumbarton Castle, except the 14th-century entrance. Most of the remains are 18th and 19th century fortifications. With a long and turbulent history from ancient times, Dumbarton became a royal castle, and was a formidable fortress, used as a place of refuge and a prison.

The infant Mary was kept at Dumbarton before being taken to France. James Douglas, Earl of Morton and Regent at one time, was imprisoned here before his execution in 1581 for his part in the murder of Darnley.

One story is that the castle terrace is haunted by the headless apparition of a sentry, mostly seen on clear moonlit nights.

Open all year: Apr-Sep, daily 9.30-18.50; Oct, daily 9.30-16.30; Nov-Mar, Sat-Wed 9.30-16.30; closed 25/26 Dec and 1/2 Jan.

Historic Scotland. Parking. Shop. Refreshments. WC. Admission charged.
01389 732167. www.historic-scotland.gov.uk

DUNBAR CASTLE

Off A1087, Dunbar, on N shore just W of harbour, East Lothian. (EH42 1WG)

Although once one of the most important castles in Scotland, little remains of Dunbar Castle, except foundations of a very ruined keep and courtyard. The ruins date in part from the 12th century. Black Agnes, Agnes Randolph, Countess of Dunbar, held the castle successfully for six weeks in 1338 against English armies. Much of the building was demolished in the 19th century to build the harbour.

In 1566, two days after Rizzio's death, Mary and Darnley arrived here – although he had been responsible for the murder. In 1567 ten weeks after Darnley was himself murdered, Mary was brought here after being abducted by Bothwell, who was the keeper of the castle. She, perhaps rather foolishly, later married him. The castle was surrendered and was destroyed after Mary had fled to England.

A ghost, known as Black Aggie, is said to have been witnessed here, only seen on clear nights.

Access at all reasonable times – care should be taken as dangerously ruined.
Parking nearby.

DUNDRENNAN ABBEY

On A711, 6 miles SE of Kirkcudbright, Dundrennan, Dumfries and Galloway. (DG6 4QH)
The fine ruins of a Cistercian abbey in a quiet and picturesque place, founded in 1142 by David I and dedicated to the Blessed Virgin Mary. Substantial parts of the church, chapter house and cloister survive.

Mary very likely spent her last night 15-16 May 1568 in Scotland at Dundrennan before sailing to England.

No stories have been found about ghosts at Dundrennan.

Open Apr–Sep, daily 9.30-17.30; Oct–Mar open wknds only 9.30-16.30; closed 25-26 Dec and 1-2 Jan.
Historic Scotland. Parking. Shop. WC. Reasonable disabled access. Admission charged.
01557 500262. www.historic-scotland.gov.uk

DUNNOTTAR CASTLE

Off A92, 2 miles S of Stonehaven, Kincardine & Deeside. (AB3 2TL)
Built on a promontory on cliffs high above the sea, Dunnottar Castle is a spectacular ruined courtyard castle of the Keith Earls Marischal, parts of which date from the 12th century, and covers a large site. The entrance and tunnel up to the castle are especially impressive.

Mary stayed here in 1562 during a progress.

Stories of ghosts include the apparition of a young girl, dressed in a dull plaid-type dress, the ghost of a young deer hound, and the phantom of a tall Scandinavian-looking man.

Open Easter–Oct, daily 9.00–18.00; winter Mon–Fri only, 10.00 to sunset; last admission 60 mins before closing.

Parking. Getting to the castle involves a walk, steep climb, and a steeper one back. Shop. Castle Picnic Van (Jun–mid Sep). WC. Admission charged.

01569 762173. www.dunnottarcastle.co.uk

EDINBURGH CASTLE

Off A1, in the centre of Edinburgh. (EH1 2NG)

Standing on a high rock, Edinburgh Castle was one of the strongest and most important fortresses in Scotland. The oldest building is a small Norman chapel of the early 12th century, dedicated to St Margaret, wife of Malcolm Canmore.

In 1566 Mary gave birth to the future James VI in the castle.

The castle is the home of the Scottish crown jewels, the huge 15th-century cannon Mons Meg, the Stone of Destiny, and much more.

The castle is reputedly haunted by many ghosts, including a headless drummer, a ghostly piper sent to search a tunnel leading down towards the High Street, phantoms of prisoners in the vaults, and the spectre of a dog whose remains are buried in the pets' cemetery (or a whole pack of dogs).

One account also has the place haunted by a spectre of Mary, while the esplanade has the ghost of Janet Douglas, Lady Glamis.

Open all year: Apr–Sep, daily 9.30–18.00; Oct–Mar, daily 9.30–17.00; times may be altered during Tattoo and state occasions; closed 25/26 Dec; open 1 Jan 11.00–17.00.

Historic Scotland. Limited parking. Shops. Restaurant and cafe. WC. Partial disabled access and mobility vehicle available. Admission charged.

0131 225 9846. www.edinburghcastle.gov.uk

EDZELL CASTLE

Off B966, 6 miles N of Brechin, Edzell, Angus. (DD9 7UE)

A fine tower house and castle, all now ruinous, with a large and attractive pleasance or garden dating from 1604. The castle was built by the Lindsay Earls of Crawford, and their burial aisle is nearby in Edzell kirkyard.

Mary visited the castle in 1562 during a progress.

The castle and burial vault are said to be haunted by a White Lady, reputedly the spirit of Catherine Campbell, second wife of David Lindsay, 9th Earl of Crawford. She apparently died in 1578 and is said to have been interred alive in her family vault, only escaping when a sexton tried to steal her rings.

Open Apr–Sep, daily 9.30–17.30; last entry 30 mins before closing.

Historic Scotland. Parking. Visitor centre/shop. WC. Reasonable disabled access. Admission charged. Garden.

01356 648631. www.historic-scotland.gov.uk

EILEAN DONAN CASTLE

On A87, 8 miles E of Kyle of Lochalsh, Dornie, Highland. (IV40 8DX)

One of the most beautifully situated and iconic of all Scottish castles, Eilean Donan Castle consists of complex of buildings on a small island. Although ruinous, it was completely rebuilt in the 20th century. This was a property of the Mackenzies. The castle has been used in many films, including the James Bond film *The World is Not Enough*, *Loch Ness* with Ted Danson, and *Highlander*.

The ghost of one of the Spanish troops, killed either at the castle or the nearby battle of Glen Shiel in 1719 during a Jacobite Rising, is said to haunt the castle.

Another apparition, Lady Mary, is said to haunt one of the bedrooms. There is no suggestion that this Lady Mary is Mary Queen of Scots, despite one account specifically making this assertion.

Open Mar–Nov, daily 10.00–1800, last admission 17.00; may also be open in winter: check with castle.

Parking. Gift shop. Tearoom. WC. Admission charged.
01599 555202. www.eileandonancastle.com

FALKLAND PALACE

Off A912, 10 miles N of Kirkcaldy, Falkland, Fife. (KY15 7BU)
A splendid fortified palace, remodelled in Renaissance style, with ranges of buildings around an open courtyard, dating from the 15th century. The restored cross house contains a refurbished room, reputedly the King's Room where James V (Mary's father) died in 1542. Falkland was a favourite residence of the Stewart monarchs, including Mary and James VI.

The tapestry gallery is said to be haunted by a White Lady, although she has also been described as a Grey Lady. She is said to have pined away after waiting in vain for her lover to return from battle. In at least one account this has been identified as the ghost of Mary, although it is not clear why.

Palace open Mar-Oct, Mon-Sat 10.00-17.00, Sun 13.00-17.00; shop, also open Nov-Feb: check days and hours.

National Trust for Scotland. Parking nearby. Shop. WC. Limited disabled access. Admission charged. Gardens. Real tennis court. 0844 493 2186. www.nts.org.uk

FLODDEN BATTLE SITE

Off A697, 0.25 miles west of Branxton, Flodden, Northumberland, England. (TD12 4SW)
Simply the most disastrous battle for the Scots. James IV, 12 Earls, scores of lairds and about 10,000 men were slain when they were routed by English forces. There is a monument from 1910 commemorating the battle 'to the brave of both nations'.

James IV dallied with the lady of Etal Castle before going on to Flodden, and an exhibition at the castle tells the story of the battle. (Etal Castle open Apr-Oct, daily 10.00-17.00; Nov-Mar, wknds only 10.00-16.00; 01890 820332 www.english-heritage.org.uk).

Flodden Battle site: access at all reasonable times.

Parking in Branxton village. Trail and info boards. Trail steep in places. www.flodden.net

FOTHERINGHAY CASTLE

2.5 miles N of Oundle, Fotheringhay, Northamptonshire. (PE8 5HZ)
The much reduced remains of a once strong castle, owned by David I, King of Scots, in the 12th century, along with other properties in Huntingdon. The Scots held it until 1294. Richard III of England was born here in 1452.

Towards the end of her captivity, Mary was moved to Fotheringhay and it was here that she was tried for treason and then finally beheaded on 8 February 1587. The story goes that James VI had the castle demolished, and materials from here, including the stair Mary is said to have descended on the day of her execution, were used to build the Talbot Hotel in Oundle. There is a plaque to Mary.

Open during daylight hours.

GLAMIS CASTLE

Off A94, 5.5 miles SW of Forfar, 1 mile N of Glamis village, Angus. (DD8 1RJ)
Glamis Castle is a hugely impressive and striking fortress, consisting of a greatly extended 14th-century tower with later ranges, set in an extensive park. This is the property of the Lyon Earls of Strathmore and Kinghorne. In 1540 the young and beautiful wife of the 6th Lord, Janet Douglas, was burned to death on Castle Hill of Edinburgh Castle on a suspect charge of treason, poisoning and witchcraft by James V, who hated the Douglases.

Mary visited the castle in 1562.

The castle is reputed to be one the most haunted in Britain, including by the Grey Lady of Glamis, the ghost of Janet Douglas, mentioned above. Another story is that of the ghost of a small black boy, in one account said to be the servant of Mary, although on what evidence remains unclear.

Open Mar-Dec, daily 10.00-18.00, last admission 16.30; Nov-Dec, daily: check opening times; groups at other times by appt only.

Parking. Shops. Restaurant. WC. Disabled access to gardens and ground floor. Extensive park, Pinetum, nature trail and garden. Admission charged.

01307 840393. www.glamis-castle.co.uk

HAILES CASTLE

Off A1, 4 miles E of Haddington, 1.5 miles W of East Linton, East Lothian. (EH41 4PY)
In a lovely location above the River Tyne, Hailes Castle is a picturesque ruinous castle, which dates from the 13th century, and has two pit-prisons. Hailes was long a Hepburn property, and saw much action down the centuries.

Bothwell brought Mary here after abducting her in 1567, and they married soon afterwards.

There are tales that one of the pit prisons is haunted, and of a White Lady.
Access at all reasonable times.
Historic Scotland. Parking.
www.historic-scotland.gov.uk

HAYCOCK HOTEL, WANSFORD

London Road, Wansford, Peterborough, Cambridgeshire, England. (PE8 6JA)
The popular hotel, set in the picturesque village of Wansford, began as a coaching inn in the 16th century.

Mary stayed here on her way to Fotheringhay Castle in 1587.
Her ghost is reputed to haunt the building.
Hotel.
01780 782223   www.macdonaldhotels.co.uk/our-hotels/the-haycock-hotel

HERMITAGE CASTLE

Off B6399, 5 miles N of Newcastleton, Borders. (TD9 0LU)
One of the most impressive and oppressive of Scottish fortresses, Hermitage Castle is a large brooding fortress in a bleak location. It had many owners, including the Hepburn Earls of Bothwell. In 1566 Bothwell was badly wounded in a skirmish with Wee Jock Elliot of Park,

a notorious Border reiver, and was paid a visit at Hermitage by Mary.

Ghostly screams and cries have reputedly been heard from the victims of one of the lords, Lord Soulis, and his own ghost has been reported here. The ghost of Alexander Ramsay is said to have been witnessed within the walls, as has that of Mary, clad in a white dress, seen outside the castle.

Open Apr–Sep, daily 9.30–17.30, last entry 30 mins before closing.
Historic Scotland. Parking. Shop. Admission charged.
01387 376222. www.historic-scotland.gov.uk

INCHMAHOME PRIORY

Off A91, 4 miles E of Aberfoyle, Lake of Menteith, Stirlingshire. (FK8 3RA)
Set on an idyllic wooded island in a picturesque loch are the ruins of a small Augustinian

priory, dedicated to St Colman. The priory was founded in 1238, Robert the Bruce visited the priory, and David II was married here.

Mary was sent here for safety in 1547 before leaving for France.

Open Apr–Sep, daily 10.00–17.30; October, daily 10.00–16.30; ferry subject to cancellation during bad weather; last ferry leaves one hour before closing.
Historic Scotland. Parking. Ferry to island. Gift shop. WC. Admission charged.
01877 385294. www.historic-scotland.gov.uk

KELSO ABBEY

Off A698, Kelso, Borders. (TD5 7JF)
This was one of the richest and largest monastic establishments in Scotland, yet it is much more ruinous than the other Border abbeys. Founded in the 12th century, the abbey was sacked by the English during the Rough Wooing.

Mary visited in 1566.

One story is that the bells were hidden in the Tweed to stop them being stolen by

English raiders, and that on stormy nights and in times of trouble the bells can still be heard to ring from under the waters of the Tweed.

Access at all reasonable times.

Historic Scotland. Parking nearby.

www.historic-scotland.gov.uk

LANGSIDE BATTLE SITE

Off B768, north of Langside Avenue and Battlefield Road, Queen's Park, Langside, Glasgow. (G42 9QL)

The fateful battle on 13 May 1568, when the forces of Mary were routed by an army under her half brother Moray, although the loss of life was not extensive, being about 300 on Mary's side. There is a memorial to the battle, dating from 1887.

Apparitions of men who fought here, reputedly with missing limbs and other wounds, have reputedly been seen near the boating lake and elsewhere on the anniversary of the battle.

Access at all reasonable times.

LENNOXLOVE

Off A1, between B6369 and B6368, 1 mile S of Haddington, Lennoxlove, East Lothian. (EH41 4NZ)

Originally known as Lethington, Lennoxlove is an attractive castle and mansion, which includes work from the 14th century. This was a property of Sir William Maitland, secretary to Mary. He was captured as part of Mary's garrison when Edinburgh Castle fell in 1573, and died soon afterwards, possibly by poison and to avoid being hanged.

Lennoxlove is now held by the Dukes of Hamilton.

Among the treasures it holds are the death mask of Mary, a sapphire ring given to her by Lord John Hamilton, and the casket which may have contained the Casket Letters.

Open for guided tours Easter–Oct, Wed, Thu and Sun, 13.30–15.30; check with house before visiting.

01620 828608. www.lennoxlove.com

LINLITHGOW PALACE

Off A803, in Linlithgow, West Lothian. (EH49 7AL)

A magnificent ruinous palace arranged around an open courtyard with a working fountain, which may include 12th-century work. The present building dates from the reign of James I and later became a favourite residence of the Scottish monarchs. It was accidentally burnt out in 1746 during the Jacobite Risings.

James V was born here in 1512, as was Mary in 1542.

The palace is said to be haunted by a Blue Lady. Queen Margaret's Bower, at the top of one of the stair-towers, is reputed to be haunted by the ghost of either Margaret Tudor, wife of James IV, or Mary of Guise, wife of James V.

An apparition of Mary is also reputed to have been seen, praying in the chapel.

Open all year: Apr–Sep, daily 9.30–17.30; Oct–Mar, daily 9.30–16.30; last ticket sold 45 mins before closing; closed 25/26 Dec and 1/2 Jan.

Historic Scotland. Parking. Shop. Refreshments. WC. Partial disabled access. Admission charged. 01506 842896. www.historic-scotland.gov.uk

LOCHLEVEN CASTLE

Off B996, 1 mile E of Kinross, Loch Leven, Perthshire. (KY13 8UF)

Standing on an idyllic island in a picturesque loch is a small ruinous rectangular keep, standing at one corner of a courtyard. This was a royal castle from 1257 but passed to the Douglases.

Mary was held here from 1567 until she escaped the following year, during which time she signed her abdication. She is also said to have had a miscarriage while imprisoned, losing twins. The castle is said to be haunted by Mary, reported in this case to be looking for her lost babies.

Open Apr–Sep, daily 9.30–17.30; Oct, daily 9.30–16.30; last ticket sold 60 mins before closing – includes ferry trip from Kinross.

Historic Scotland. Parking. Shop. Refreshments nearby. Admission charged. Ferry. 01577 862670. www.historic-scotland.gov.uk

LOUVRE PALACE

Musee de Louvre, 75058 Paris, France.

The huge and magnificent palace of the French kings, later enlarged and used by Napoleon. The palace houses a huge collection of art, and is entered from beneath the courtyard by a unique glass pyramid. It was in the old part of the palace that Mary was betrothed to François.

Open all year, Wed–Mon (closed Tue) and closed 1/1, 1/5 and 25/12.

Shops. Cafes. WC. Disabled access. Admission charge. www.louvre.fr

MARY QUEEN OF SCOTS VISITOR CENTRE, JEDBURGH

Off A68, Queen Street, Jedburgh, Borders. (TD8 6EN)

Situated in a fine location, the building is an interesting old tower house, dating from the 16th century. Mary stayed in a chamber on the second floor. She was ill and lay near death for many days after her visit to Bothwell at Hermitage in 1566.

The house may be haunted, although reports are vague. Whether these are linked to Mary is not known.

Open Mar–Nov, Mon–Sat 10.00–16.30, Sun 11.00–16.30.

Fascinating visitor centre with artifacts and info about Mary, including her death mask. Free. 01835 863331. www.scotborders.gov.uk

MELVILLE CASTLE

Off A7, 1.5 miles W of Dalkeith, Melville, Midlothian. (EH18 1AP)
Set in 50 acres of park and woodland, the present house, a grand baronial mansion, was built at the end of the 18th century and replaced an old castle.

This old castle was reputedly visited by Mary and may have also been used by David Rizzio on more than one occasion.

The castle is said to be haunted by either the spirit of Elizabeth Rennie, unfaithful wife to one of the owners, or perhaps by another spectre of Mary.

Available for weddings, corporate events or for exclusive use.
0131 654 0088. www.melvillecastle.com

NATIONAL MUSEUM OF SCOTLAND, EDINBURGH

Chambers Street, Edinburgh. (EH1 1JF)
This magnificent museum houses extensive collections on Scotland's history, land and people, covering the decorative arts, natural history, science and technology, working life and geology.

There are also displays associated with Mary, including furniture, jewellery, a letter, and the keys of Lochleven Castle, as well as a copy of her white marble effigy from her tomb in Westminster Abbey.

Open all year: Mon–Sat, daily 10.00–17.00; closed Christmas day.
Parking nearby. Gift shop. Tearooms and rooftop restaurant. WC. Disabled access. Free admission.
0300 123 6789. www.nms.ac.uk

NOTRE DAME CATHEDRAL

Paris, France.
Built on an island in the Seine, Notre Dame is a large and magnificent cathedral, which dates from medieval times.

Mary and François, the Dauphin of France and later king, were married here in 1558.

Open all year except during services.
www.notredamedeparis.fr

OLD HALL HOTEL, BUXTON

The Square, Buxton, Derbyshire, England. (SK17 6BD)
The New Hall, as it was once known, was built by the Earl of Shrewsbury and Bess of Hardwick, and this replaced the Old Hall, although that is how the building is now known. This was in turn incorporated into a new house in the 18th century.

Mary was held here, although it was a welcome change to some of her other prisons. She was at times lavishly entertained during her visits, and this apparently annoyed Elizabeth. Mary scratched her famous couplet of Farewell to Buxton with a diamond ring on one of the bedroom window panes, writing:

'Buxton, whose warm waters have made thy name famous, perchance I shall visit thee no more-Farewell.'

Vague stories suggest that the building is haunted, and some people have claimed that they have felt Mary's presence in Room 26.

Hotel.
01298 22841. www.oldhallhotelbuxton.co.uk

Old Hall, Buxton (see previous page)

PALACE OF HOLYROODHOUSE, EDINBURGH

Off A1, at foot of Royal Mile, in Edinburgh. (EH8 8DX)

The official residence of the monarch in Scotland, the Palace of Holyroodhouse is an impressive and historic palace, ranged round a courtyard, with one towered block dating from the 16th century. The building was remodelled and extended for Charles II in 1671-8, but original 16th-century interiors survive in the old block.

David Rizzio, Mary's secretary, was murdered here in 1566 in front of the pregnant queen. His body was dumped and it is said that the blood from his murder cannot to be removed from the floor, despite repeated attempts to clean it.

A Grey Lady, thought to be the spirit of one of Mary's companions, has reputedly been seen in the Queen's Audience Chamber. Another female ghost is reportedly Bald Agnes, thought to be the spirit of Agnes Sampson who was accused of witchcraft by James VI and executed in 1591.

The fine ruins of the abbey church adjoin the palace, and can also be visited. The church is the burial place of James V and others of the Royal family, although the tombs were despoiled by the English in their attacks of 1544 and 1547.

Open all year (except during royal visits): Apr-Oct, daily 9.30-18.00; Nov-Mar, daily 9.30-16.30; closed 25-26 Dec.

Parking nearby. Gift shop. Cafe. WC. Disabled access. Admission charged.
0131 556 5100. www.royalcollection.org.uk

PETERBOROUGH CATHEDRAL

Minster Precincts, Peterborough, England. (PE1 1XS)
One of the finest cathedrals in England, with a history that goes back 900 years, although there was an older establishment on the site. The church was part of a Benedictine monastery, but after the Reformation became the cathedral for the new diocese of Peterborough.

Catherine of Aragon, Henry VIII's first wife, is buried here, as was Mary after her body had been left at Fotheringhay for some months. James VI had Mary reinterred in Westminster Abbey in 1612.

Peterborough Cathedral is also said to be haunted, with an apparition of a little girl who was apparently murdered, the ghosts of monks and a stone mason, and the sounds of an unseen choir.
Open all year, daily.
Parking. Shop. Coffee shop. WC. Disabled access.
01733 355300. www.peterborough-cathedral.org.uk

PINKIE BATTLE SITE

Just off A6094, 0.5 miles south of Wallyford, just north of junction with A1. (EH21 8QH)
The site of the Battle of Pinkie on Black Saturday, 10 September 1547, where a Scottish army led by the Earl of Arran was routed with heavy losses by the English under Protector Somerset. This was part of the Rough Wooing, which was certainly rough yet ultimately unsuccessful. There is a memorial just off the A6094.
Access to monument at all reasonable times.

SCOTTISH NATIONAL PORTRAIT GALLERY, EDINBURGH

1 Queen Street, Edinburgh. (EH2 1JD)
The gallery building, designed by the architect Sir Robert Rowand Anderson in the 1880s, resembles a Florentine palace. The gallery provides a visual history of Scotland from the 16th century to the present day. Among the most famous are Mary, Ramsay's portrait of David Hume and Raeburn's Sir Walter Scott. Other artists include Van Dyck, Gainsborough, Copley, Rodin, Kokoschka and Torvaldsen.

The building also houses the Scottish National Collection of Photography.
Open all year, daily 10.00-17.00, also Thu until 19.00; extended hours during Festival; closed 25 Dec-1 Jan.
Parking nearby. Gift shop. Cafe. WC. Disabled access and WC. Free admission except for special exhibitions.
0131 6246200. www.nationalgalleries.org/portraitgallery

SHEFFIELD MANOR LODGE

Off A57 (Sheffield Parkway), 1 mile east of Sheffield city centre. (S2 1UL)
The sprawling but mostly very ruinous remains of Manor Lodge, apart from the magnificent Turret House. This was once one of the grandest manor houses in the north of England, and was held by the Earls of Shrewsbury.

Mary was held here at various times, and it is said that her ghost haunts Manor Lodge.
Access at all reasonable times. Guided tours of Turret House. Check with site for days and times.
Parking. Cafes. WC. Partial disabled access.
01142 762828. www.manorlodge.org.uk

SPYNIE PALACE

Off A941, 2.5 miles N of Elgin, Spynie, Moray. (IV30 5QG)

One of the finest castles in Scotland, the palace consists of a massive keep, Davy's Tower, at one corner of a large courtyard, enclosing ranges of buildings. All are now ruinous. The

palace was probably built by Bishop Innes, after Elgin Cathedral had been burnt by the Wolf of Badenoch. There are fine views from the tower.

Mary visited in 1562, as did Bothwell in 1567 after he had fled from Carberry Hill. He moved on to Orkney, and from there the continent where he was imprisoned by the King of Denmark.

There were stories of the bishops being in league with the Devil, and that every Halloween witches would be seen flying to the castle. The castle is also reputedly haunted, and unexplained lights and unearthly music are said to have been witnessed here. There are also stories of a phantom piper, the spectre of a woman, and a ghostly lion.

Open Apr-Sep, daily 9.30-17.30; Oct-Mar, wknds only 9.30-16.30; closed 25/26 Dec and 1/2 Jan.

Historic Scotland. Parking. Gift shop. WC. Admission charged. Joint ticket with Elgin Cathedral available.
01343 546358. www.historic-scotland.gov.uk

ST ANDREWS CASTLE

Off A91, St Andrews, Fife. (KY16 9AR)

A ruined courtyard castle, enclosed by a wall with a gatehouse and towers, one of which contains a bottle dungeon cut into the rock. The first castle here was built by Bishop Roger, and it was held by the bishops and archbishops. In 1546 a band of Protestants murdered Cardinal David Beaton, and hung his naked body from one of the towers. There are tunnels from the resultant siege, which can be entered and are some of the finest siege works in Europe.

A dubious tale is that a phantom of Bothwell has allegedly been seen, but as a young man. The story goes that he was held in the castle while accusation against him were being investigated.

The ghost of Archbishop John Hamilton, one of Mary's supporters, who was hanged at Stirling, is said to haunt the castle; some reports have Cardinal David Beaton's apparition also being seen here, and the spectre of Archbishop James Sharp being seen in a carriage in St Andrews. There are also tales of a White Lady, seen near the stronghold and on the nearby beach, possibly the same spectre as more often witnessed in and around the cathedral. She has been described as being clad in white with a veil which obscures her face.

Open all year: Apr-Sep, daily 9.30-17.30; Oct-Mar, daily 9.30-16.30; closed 25/26 Dec and check New Year.

Historic Scotland. Parking nearby. Shop. WC. Partial disabled access. Admission charged. Joint ticket with St Andrews Cathedral available.
01334 477196. www.historic-scotland.gov.uk

ST MARY'S GUILDHALL, COVENTRY

Bayley Lane, Coventry, England. (CV1 5RN)
The guildhall, which is more than 650 years old, is the finest in the country, and has ranges of buildings, including the magnificent great hall with a minstrels' gallery, around a courtyard. It is thought that William Shakespeare may have staged plays here, and there is a cafe in the vaulted undercroft. Much of the building is open to the public, while some rooms are used as offices.

Mary was held here from late 1569 until early 1570, in what is known as the Mary Queen of Scots' Room, during a Catholic rising in the north of England. She then went on to Tutbury.

The building is said to be haunted: the manifestations have not (so far anyway) been linked to Mary.

Open mid March-early October, Sunday-Thursday (check with site for exact dates).

Parking nearby. Cafe. WC. Partial disabled access.
0247 683 3328. www.stmarysguildhall.co.uk

STIRLING CASTLE

Off A872, Upper Castle Hill, in Stirling. (FK8 1EJ)
One of the most important and powerful castles in Scotland with a long and violent history, the castle stands on a high rock with fine views, and consists of a very impressive complex of buildings, including the restored Great Hall and the Chapel Royal. Other features of interest are the kitchens, the wall walk and the nearby King's Knot.

The infant Mary was crowned in the old chapel in 1543, and the future James VI was baptised here in 1566.

The Pink Lady, the apparition of a beautiful woman, has reputedly been seen at the castle, and some have suggested that this is ghost of Mary. The Green Lady's appearance is a harbinger of ill news, often associated with fire. There are also many reports of ghostly footsteps in more than one area of the castle, and reports of a kilted apparition, photographed in 1935 and seen afterwards.

Open all year: Apr-Sep daily 9.30-18.00; Oct-Mar daily 9.30-17.00; closed 25/26 Dec; open 1/2 Jan: tel for opening times.

Historic Scotland. Parking. Shops. Cafe. WC. Disabled access. Admission charged.
01786 450000. www.stirlingcastle.gov.uk

Stirling Castle, Great Hall (see previous page)

TALBOT HOTEL, OUNDLE

New Street, Oundle, Northamptonshire, England. (PE8 4EA)
The hotel was partly built with materials from Fotheringhay Castle, including the oak staircase Mary is said to have descended before being executed.

Her ghost is reputed to haunt the hotel, having apparently been translated, along with the stair, windows and other material, from Fotheringhay. Manifestations are said to increase in February.
Hotel.
01832 273621. www.thetalbot-oundle.com

TANTALLON CASTLE

Off A198, 3 miles E of North Berwick, Tantallon, East Lothian. (EH39 5PN)
One of the most impressive castles in southern Scotland, Tantallon is a large and strong 14th-century courtyard castle, which is now ruinous. It has a thick 80-foot-high curtain wall, blocking off a high promontory, with towers at each end and a central gatehouse. The castle was built by the Douglases, later Earls of Angus, and has a long and violent history. It was besieged by James V in 1528 but did not fall.

Mary visited in 1566.

A photograph taken in the castle, showing what many believe is a ghost at an old doorway to a turnpike stair, was widely reported in the media, although it may have just been a visitor to the castle.
Open Apr-Sep, daily 9.30-17.30; Oct-Mar, daily 9.30-16.30; closed 25/26 Dec and 1/2 Jan.

Historic Scotland. Parking (walk to castle). Shop. WC. Limited disabled access.
Admission charged.
01620 892727 www.historic-scotland.gov.uk

TIXALL HALL GATEHOUSE

Tixall Mews, Tixall, Stafford, Staffordshire, England. (ST18 0XT)
Although the impressive Elizabethan mansion is gone, and also its successor, the imposing gatehouse still survives. This was built by the Aston family in the middle of the 16th century. The gate house was refurbished and can be rented as holiday accommodation.

Mary was held at Tixall in August 1586 while her quarters at Chartley Manor were being searched for evidence of treason against Elizabeth.

There are some stories that the gatehouse is haunted, but not apparently by Mary.
The gatehouse can be rented as holiday accommodation.
01628 825920. www.landmarktrust.org.uk

TOWER OF LONDON

London, England. (EC3N 4AB)
The Tower of London is one of the foremost tourist attractions in Britain, and has a long, fascinating and bloody history, not least during the reigns of the Tudors.

One interesting tale, but perhaps a little flimsy even for a ghost story, is that the spirit of Mary is heard wailing to herald the death of the British monarch. This terrible noise was apparently heard three times on Christmas Eve in 1900, a few weeks before the death of Queen Victoria. Mary never visited the Tower or had any connection with it.

There were many executions at the Tower in the 16th century and later, not least

153

Catherine Howard, Lady Jane Grey, Anne Boleyn, Thomas Howard, Duke of Norfolk, and Robert Devereux, Earl of Essex, formerly Elizabeth's favourite and one of Mary's jailers.

Open all year, except 24–26 Dec and I Jan.

Shops. Cafes. WC. Admission price. Disabled access.

0844 4827777. www.hrp.org.uk/TowerOfLondon/

TRAQUAIR HOUSE

Off B709, 1 mile S of Innerleithen, Borders. (EH44 6PW)

Reputedly the oldest continuously occupied house in Scotland, Traquair House dates from as early as the 12th century. The striking white-washed castle and mansion houses a collection of mementoes associated with Mary, who stayed here with Darnley and the infant future James VI in 1566. In the museum is Mary's rosary and crucifix and a letter signed by her, and in the King's Room is the bed she slept in at Terregles House on her flight to England, and a wooden cradle used by James.

Traquair House is not believed to be haunted, and this is apparently not one of the places that Mary's busy spirit frequents.

Open early Apr–late Oct, daily: Apr–Sep, 11.00–17.00; Oct, 11.00–16.00; Nov, open Sat & Sun only 11.00–15.00

Parking. Shop. Restaurant. WC. Admission charge. Partial disabled access. Extensive grounds. Brewery.

01896 830323. www.traquair.co.uk

TUTBURY CASTLE

Off A511, Castle Street, Tutbury, Staffordshire. (DE13 9JF)

The fine sprawling ruins of a substantial castle and manor, which dates from 1071 as the Normans spread across England after Hastings. The castle was used by John of Gaunt, 2nd Duke of Lancaster, and was besieged several times before being dismantled in 1647-48 after holding out for Charles I.

Mary was imprisoned here four times, and this was the place that she hated the most.

Her ghost is said to haunt the castle. One of the most interesting occasions is when an

apparition clad in white was seen around midnight in the South Tower by some 40 members of the armed services.

Another ghost is reputed to be seen clad in a full set of armour, and to tell visitors to 'get thee hence' or to leave the place.

Open April-end September, Tue-Sun 11.00-17.00, closed Mon except for Bank Holidays.

Parking. Tearoom. Shop. WC. Admission charge. Limited disabled access. Garden.
01283 812129. www.tutburycastle.com

WEMYSS CASTLE GARDENS

Off A955, 3 miles NE of Kirkcaldy, Wemyss, Fife. (KY1 4TE)
Wemyss Castle is a large rambling castle and mansion, situated above the sea, a property of the Wemyss family, later Earls of Wemyss. Charles II visited in 1650 and 1651, but the family were forfeited for their part in the Jacobite Rising of 1745, although the title was restored in 1826.

Mary first met Darnley here in 1565, and the family fought for her at Langside in 1568.

A Green Lady or Green Jean reputedly haunts the castle.

Gardens may be visited by prior appointment only, May-Jul, Mon-Fri only, 9.30-18.00; castle not open.

Parking nearby. Partial disabled access. Admission charged.
01592 652181. wemysscastlegardens.com

WESTMINSTER ABBEY, LONDON

Westminster (opposite Houses of Parliament), London, England. (SW1P 3PA)
The magnificent abbey church is the burial place of Mary. Her tomb had been in Peterborough Cathedral after her execution in 1587, but James VI had her remains brought to Westminster Abbey and reinterred in the Lady Chapel and he built a magnificent tomb

Lady Chapel, Westminster Abbey

(much larger and about twice as expensive as Elizabeth's) with a white marble effigy of his mother under an elaborate canopy.

There are a couple of ghost stories. One is about a ghost known as Father Benedictus, a phantom clad in a cowl, seen floating slightly above the present ground level in the cloister. The spectre of a man in World War I uniform is reported to have been witnessed beside the tomb of the unknown soldier.

Open all year except Sundays and festivals.

Parking nearby. Cafe. Shop. WC. Admission charge. Disabled access.
020 7222 5152. www.westminster-abbey.org

WINGFIELD MANOR

Off A615, South Wingfield, Alfreton, Derbyshire, England. (DE55 7NH)
A huge and monumentally impressive ruin of a manor house and tower, built by Ralph, Lord Cromwell, Treasurer of England. By the reign of Elizabeth it was held by the Earls of Shrewsbury.

Mary was held here, and this is another place she is said to haunt. The ghost is said to be especially active at specific times of the year, and one reported manifestation is blue flickering lights seen in the undercroft. This activity may relate to the murder of a maid in this part of the building in the 17th century by a rival in love. One story is that all the ghostly activity led to the manor being abandoned.

Guided tours on 1st Sat of the month, April–September: call to confirm.

English Heritage. Parking nearby (300 yards). Admission price. Part of a working farm.
0870 333 1181. www.english-heritage.org.uk

WORKINGTON HALL

On A66, Curwen Park, E of Workington, Cumbria. (CA14 4BP)
The ruins of an elegant old house and fortress of the Curwen family, who held the property until 1929. Mary stayed at Workington Hall for one night in 1568 after fleeing from Dundrennan by boat. From here she wrote to Elizabeth, expressing fears for her safety. Soon after Mary was held in Carlisle Castle. Mary gave Sir Henry Curwen a goblet fashioned from agate, which became known as the Luck of Workington.

The hall is said to be haunted by the ghost of a later Henry Curwen, a Jacobite, who died in mysterious circumstances in 1725. Unexplained thumping on a stair and elsewhere in the building were reported.

Hall ruins not currently open but grounds and park are accessible.

01900 702510. www.allerdale.gov.uk

INDEX